JUST
BEFORE
SUNSET

by
Lora L. Cline

Just Before Sunset
Sunbelt Publications, Inc
Copyright © 1984 by Lora L. Cline
All rights reserved. Third edition 2008

Cover revision and book design by Leah Cooper
Project management by Jennifer Redmond
Printed in the United States of America

Sunbelt Publications, Inc.
P.O. Box 191126
San Diego, CA 92159-1126
(619) 258-4911, fax: (619) 258-4916
www.sunbeltbooks.com

11 10 09 08   5 4 3 2 1

Library of Congress Cataloging-in-Publication Data

Cline, Lora L.
  Just before sunset / by Lora L. Cline. -- 3rd ed.
     p. cm.
  Includes bibliographical references.
  ISBN 978-0-932653-87-1
  1. Diegueño Indians--Social life and customs. 2. Lucas, Tom, 1903- 3. Diegueño Indians--Biography. I. Title.
  E99.D5C58 2008
  979.4'00497572--dc22
                          2008010207

Original cover design by Timothy Reel.
Old photographs, unless otherwise noted, are from Tom Lucas' collection. Other photographs are by the author.

Dedicated to the memory of my friend,
Tom Lucas

Contents

         Housing Settlements, Trade and Trails
         Trail Shrines
         Hunting
         Weapons, Tools and Fishing
         Nets
         Food Gathering and Preparation
         Basketry
         Pottery
         Mortars
         Beverages
         Agriculture

         Clothing
         Hair
         Jewelry
         Tattoos
         Social Dances
         Musical Instruments
         Toys
         Games
         Animals and Pets

List of Illustrations

Preface to the Third Edition

My meeting and association with Tom Lucas afforded me the opportunity to record a significant quantity of valuable information he remembered about his people. At first, it was simply many hours of me asking him questions, with him waiting patiently while I recorded his answers. After the initial recording sessions at his home in Pacific Beach, he invited me to the Lucas Ranch (formerly the *Kwaaymii* Indian Reservation) in the Laguna Mountains, to see the homeland he had been telling me about.

Ultimately, we developed a close friendship, one that would span several years. In addition to our recording sessions, we spent many hours just visiting, talking not just about the *Kwaaymii* but about other subjects as well. During those visits, I turned my tape recorder off, or didn't take it with me at all. Tom's daughters, Susaan and Carmen, lived at the ranch, and we also had many good times together. Tom often entertained us all with his marvelous sense of humor.

There have been many requests to reprint this book, and I am grateful the opportunity has arisen for a new edition to be published. I hope the reader will appreciate the dedication Tom Lucas had to recording the history of his *Kwaaymii* ancestors.

Lora L. Cline
Spring, 2008

Preface to the Second Edition

Continued demand required that this unduplicated story be republished. Though it quickly became a standard reference work on the mountain *Kumeyaay* of Southern California, research questions that the first edition promoted also required that some revisions be made for the second issue. The result is a more complete work. Like the first edition, this book—recast as *Just Before Sunset*—is highly reflective of Lora Cline's skillful literary management as well as her sensitive feeling for a man and his world that time and history would otherwise have taken from us without notice. The effort of Lora Cline and the cooperative interest of her informant, Tom Lucas, deserve the thanks of all readers and users of this book. Because of them, *Just Before Sunset* will always illumine a soft glow on the horizon of late Southern California prehistory.

Jay von Werlhof
Imperial Valley College Museum
27 February 1984

Acknowledgements

I would like to thank the following people for their help and support: Ken Hedges, Curator, San Diego Museum of Man, for his help with botany identification; Jay von Werlhof, Curator, Imperial Valley College Museum, for his guidance and encouragement; my brother, William Weitz, for his editing; Jaime Servin, I.V.C. Museum; Tom's family; my family and friends, and especially Joseph Geier.

I have included in this edition the original drawings by Tom's daughter, SuSaan Garcia (now deceased), which she had contributed for the first edition. SuSaan was a talented Native American artist.

Tom Lucas surveys his *Kwaaymii* homeland.

Introduction

The *Kwaaymii* of the Laguna Mountains were a sub-tribe of a larger group of Indians who at one time inhabited the southernmost section of California. Their territory extended from the coast to the Colorado River and along the Gila River in Arizona, north to Fish Creek, and south to just below the Mexican border. The coastal people became known as the Diegueño or Mission Indians, the eastern people the *Kwichaan* or Yuma, and those located in the central area between the two were called *Kumeyaay*. The *Kumeyaay* are divided somewhat further. The people in the higher elevations, such as the Laguna Mountains, are more closely related, culturally and linguistically, with those groups on the coast and farther north. The lower elevation *Kumeyaay* are more closely linked with the eastern desert peoples. The cultural similarities between sub-tribes are evident. Their network of trading trails not only took them from coast to river, but northward to Shoshone tribes.

The Diegueño, Yuma and *Kumeyaay* speak many varying dialects of the Yuman linguistic stock (Hokan language group). All the words of the *Kwaaymii* dialect used in this edition have been set in italics (see appendices for word pronunciation key).

The elevation of the *Kwaaymii* mountain habitat is 5,500 to 6,000 feet. The area is abundant in pine, juniper and several types of oak. Elderberry, lilac, scrub oak and many smaller varieties of vegetation grow there. The winter desert area to

xiii

which they migrated in Mason Valley is about 1,800 to 2,000 feet above sea level. Game was plentiful, and the *Kwaaymii* fully exploited their resources in the mountains and desert. They hunted Bighorn sheep, deer, rabbits, migrating ducks and geese, and at one time, bear. Water from natural springs was ample.

Some historical accounts of the white man's advance and his encounter with the Indian would have us believe that suddenly, to the Indian's surprise and chagrin, the white man was here. Quite the opposite was true according to Tom Lucas. The Indian did know the white man was coming and the role of the shaman, or medicine man, had a great deal to do with it. The shaman foretold the coming of the Spanish, the European's movement across the United States, World War I and other prophecies of lesser magnitude but of importance to the *Kwaaymii*. The villagers relied heavily on the shaman's guidance and ability to perceive the "spirit worlds." It was the shaman who knew when to plant and harvest, where the game was, when the first snows would come, and other seasonal facts important to *Kwaaymii* life.

Every aspect of *Kwaaymii* society was remarkably well organized—religious, political, social and economic. The society was patrilocal and patrilineal, meaning that a young married woman went to live in her husband's village and she and any children then became known by her husband's family name and/or his clan affiliation. Mr. Lucas recalled little of his people's clan system, only that he remembers some mention of it by elderly village members.

Although there is only one *Kwaaymii* member remaining now, the few who had survived to the early 1900s had been able to adjust to the new culture that was quickly absorbing the old. One would suspect that the shaman played a part in their ability to cope, if in fact he did predict the culture change for which they were able to prepare. Some native aboriginal cultures were completely lost to the advance of the white man. Elder members of some tribes realized the futility of passing on tribal traditions to the youngsters. Others could not cope with the pressured change. Indian populations were decimated by disease and famine.

It is fortunate, in this late twentieth century, that a few Indians have been able to keep the traditions and customs of their peoples vividly alive so that they can be recorded for future generations. It is my hope that we can all understand and enjoy the richness of the nearly forgotten Native American cultures.

Lora L. Cline
Jacumba, California

Drawing by SuSaan Garcia

Chapter I

A BIOGRAPHICAL SKETCH
OF TOM LUCAS

 TOMUS LUGO—TOM LUCAS—WAS BORN on 20 February 1903 at Laguna Indian Reservation during a heavy snow storm. His parents gave him the Indian name of *Tomus*, which means everything obliterated or covered over. He was the last *Kwaaymii* baby to be born.

The 1860 smallpox outbreak and the 1918 influenza epidemic had taken a heavy toll of the *Kwaaymii* people. Out of the three original villages, only a handful of people remained, and they all lived in the village called *Kwaaymii*. Tom had no youngsters his age to play with in the vicinity, so the elders entertained and educated him with stories of the past. The older people saw in Tom the only possibility of continuing the *Kwaaymii* heritage. Men and women both told him all they could pass on about their people's customs and beliefs. Tom has made bows and arrows, pottery, pipes, rattles, fire drills and game sticks. He has tanned skins, gathered herbs, and much more.

1

Tom with his first "white man's thunder bow and arrow." c. 1915

When Tom was about ten years old his mother was able to enroll him in the school at Descanso, California, rather than the Indian school which was located a much greater distance away from their home. He could speak no more than half a dozen English words but was eager to learn. His Indian-Spanish name, *Tomus* Lugo, was changed at the time of his baptism to the Spanish, Tomas Lugo, and then changed again when his teacher enrolled him with the closest sounding English equivalent, Thomas Lucas, which is his legal name today.

Although Tom was a bit apprehensive in his new environment, he was well accepted by the other students. They were children of ranchers for whom Tom's mother and grandmother had worked, and the family was respected by whites and Indians alike. Tom later worked for ranchers in the area to help support his mother and grandmother when he was not in school. By the time he was 21 he was on his own—the last *Kwaaymii*.

Tom competed in many rodeos when he was in his 20s. Here he is riding "War Cloud" at the Salinas Rodeo, 1926.

3

Tom and his son plowing the field, 1929.

Tom was married in 1927. He built a log house on the
reservation where he and his family lived for several years.
Realizing the importance of education, Tom and his wife pur-
chased a home in San Diego so their children could attend
school there. Tom spent an unrecalled amount of time in adult
education classes over several years, studying to better himself and his opportunities. He now divides his time between
his San Diego home and his mountain homeland. He has four
children, seven grandchildren and two great-grandchildren.

The United States government hired him as foreman in the
Civilian Conservation Corps, building roads through Indian
reservations during the 1930s in San Bernardino, Riverside,
San Diego and Imperial counties. During this time Tom made
many friends all over Southern California. Later, he was in-
volved with the construction of Camp Pendleton Marine
Corps Base. After that, the Hazard contracting firm of San
Diego employed him and he retired from there in 1974.

Tom Lucas managed to do very well in coping with the
rapidly changing times. As the last full-blooded descendant
of the *Kwaaymii*, the government deeded the Laguna Indian
Reservation to him, and it is known today as the Lucas
Ranch.

Tom Lucas—c. 1933.

Tom as foreman of Indian crews building roads through reservations, 1933.

Chapter II

ECONOMICS

Housing

BEFORE THE SPANISH INFLUENCE, *Kwaaymii* houses were circular. In the mountains they used support poles of either pine or juniper, anchored into the ground to depths of 35-40 cm. (about 15 in.). The poles, which were hardly more than large branches in the earlier style housing, were cut to desired length, and the bark was burned off. They were then placed in a circle about 30 cm. (1 ft.) apart with a small opening for an entrance. The average height of the houses was 1½ meters (4-5 ft.), and just roomy enough inside for the family to sleep. Occasionally, if the weather was bad, they cooked inside over a fire pit located in the center of the dwelling.

Upright support poles were tied together at the top by fiber ropes. Then pine boughs were attached and secured starting at the bottom and working upwards, overlapping the previously placed layer. Doors were made of either hide or woven reeds and were attached by buckskin thongs or fiber rope.

Earlier winter housing in Mason Valley was built similarly, but support poles were mesquite and sometimes pine (which had to be transported from the mountain area). Coverings included arrowweed, mesquite, reeds, or any suitable desert

Old type circular housing structure, Hapaha Flat, Pinyon Mountains. In foreground are Bighorn sheep horns, flat grinding slab with hand stone, and broken pottery. c. 1932.

flora. In the Mason Valley area, entrances faced either east, southeast or south to protect the dwellers from prevailing west winds and to afford them as much light as possible. Sometimes there were two entrances.

Windows were occasionally used. They were made of a thinly shaved hide, stretched over a frame and tied in place with deer hide thongs. Although the camps in Mason Valley were only temporary winter quarters, the housing was made sturdier than mountain dwellings to counter the strong, cold desert winds.

The later style housing was square shaped and better built. Large forked poles were anchored upright in the four corners with cross beams fitted and secured to the upright forks. Additional straight poles were sunk into the ground and tied to the cross beams to support the wall structure and roof.

Smaller poles were secured horizontally affording even more support and something more stable on which to attach

10

A blending of cultures—the old style ramada built onto Maria's newer house. c. 1908.

11

the outer coverings. This style housing lasted about one hundred years, from the late 1700s to late 1800s.

Most families built their houses in close proximity to each other. It was not unusual to find the children of related families all eating together—family ties were close. The poles for housing used in mountain and desert areas lasted several years, although the siding usually had to be replaced each year. When a house was no longer suitable or useful, it was simply burned down and another built over the same spot. The *Kwaaymii* sometimes used a type of plaster made from clay and pine resin on the outside of the house for added protection. Families always moved back into the place in which they had previously lived, whether it was in a permanent mountain or temporary desert house. The tool used to dig the holes for upright poles was called the *kullmataw*. It was paddle or shovel shaped from hard wood, usually mesquite. A type of shelter rarely used was a lean-to. A person living alone might build this type of structure, but it was unsuitable for family use.

Until the *Kwaaymii* began losing their "abandoned" homeland in the mountains to cattlemen, all occupants of the three villages migrated seasonally to the desert. But from the mid-1800s the housing was more sturdily built, and a few people then stayed behind through the winter months to protect their homeland from the usurpers. Tom was born in the mountains the winter of 1903.

Settlements, Trade and Trails

The permanent *Kwaaymii* settlement was located where the Lucas Ranch is today at Mt. Laguna, California. There were originally three main villages. The largest was known as *Iiahkaay*, meaning wooded area across a meadow. It is estimated, through stories handed down, that there may have been several hundred people occupying this village at one time. Three quarters of a mile south of *Iiahkaay* was the village of *Kwaaymii*, the last occupied village and the one in which Tom Lucas was born. This village was named after the leg-

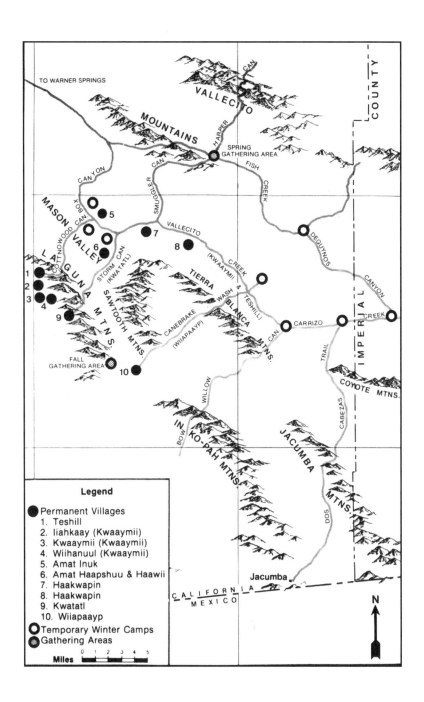

TO WARNER SPRINGS

VALLECITO

MOUNTAINS

HARPER CAN.

SPRING
GATHERING AREA

FISH CREEK

CANYON

SMUGGLER CAN.

BOX CAN.

VALLECITO

5

MASON VALLEY

6

COTTONWOOD CAN.

7

8

CREEK

(KWAAYMII)

DEGUYNOS CANYON

L A G U N A

STORM CAN.
(KWATATL)

TIERRA

(KWAAYMII & TESHILL)

1
2
3

SAWTOOTH MTNS.

BLANCA

WASH

CARRIZO

IMPERIAL

CREEK

4

9

CANEBRAKE
(WIIAPAAYP)

MTNS.

CAN.

TRAIL

COYOTE MTNS.

FALL
GATHERING AREA

10

WILLOW

CABEZAS

IN KO-PAH MTNS.

BOW

JACUMBA

DOS

MTNS.

Jacumba

N

CALIFORNIA
MEXICO

COUNTY

Legend

● Permanent Villages
1. Teshill
2. Iiahkaay (Kwaaymii)
3. Kwaaymii (Kwaaymii)
4. Wiihanuul (Kwaaymii)
5. Amat Inuk
6. Amat Haapshuu & Haawii
7. Haakwapin
8. Haakwapin
9. Kwatatl
10. Wiiapaayp
○ Temporary Winter Camps
◉ Gathering Areas

0 1 2 3 4 5
Miles

endary *Kwaaymii* bird which lived at the spring common to all the villages (see Chapter VII). The legend is that the bird arose from the spring and revealed itself to those who had spiritual vision to warn villagers of impending perils. Tom claims to have seen the *Kwaaymii* bird before his grandmother died in 1917.

About one quarter mile southeast of the *Kwaaymii* village was the *Wiihanull* (flat rock) village. Tom's grandmother remembered at least twenty families living there. About 1825 some ill fate befell *Wiihanull* and all the inhabitants died suddenly. It was speculated that they died from food poisoning. Tom was warned as a child to stay away from the old village.

The closest neighbors to the north of the *Kwaaymii* people were the *Teshill*. They abandoned their village about the time the Birch Overland Mail Route was established and migrated to the Green Valley area. The neighbors to the south were the *Kwatatl*, who abandoned the rancheria at Laguna Meadow area about 1865 and moved to the Los Conejos Indian Reservation. Southeast of the *Kwatatl* people were the *Wiiapaayp*

Tom stands at the sign marking the Birch Overland Mail Route at the top of Cottonwood Canyon. The *Teshill* people who lived there vacated their village when the mail route was established in 1857.

14

(leaning rock) whose area today is the Cuyapaipe Indian Reservation. Although the *Kwaaymii* and the *Teshill* used the Cottonwood Canyon trail to Mason Valley, they did not camp together. The *Teshill* were considered to be a different people. The *Kwaaymii* call the trail *wiipuk uun'yaw* (desert path). The temporary winter campsites *(ahktaa)* were mostly at the base of the canyon in the southwest portion of Mason Valley. The permanent village and the people who lived there were called the *Amat Inuk*. Sometimes a few *Kwaaymii* would go to the coast to camp near friends or relatives which served a dual purpose—winter camping and trading.

The *Kwatatl* people used Storm Canyon for their temporary winter migration. They camped in the area known today as the Spencer Ranch in the westernmost section of Vallecito Valley. There was a permanent village there known as *Amat Haapshuu*. Tom's great-grandmother came from that village. The *Wiiapaayp* people moved down the Canebrake Wash to Palm Spring, not far from Vallecito Creek. All the groups men-

Arnat Inuk, Mason Valley, winter quarters for the *Kwaaymii*

15

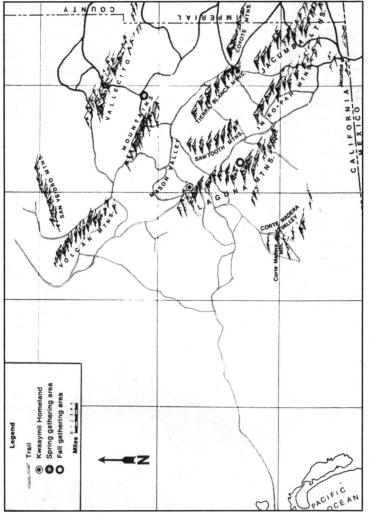

Trail System for San Diego County

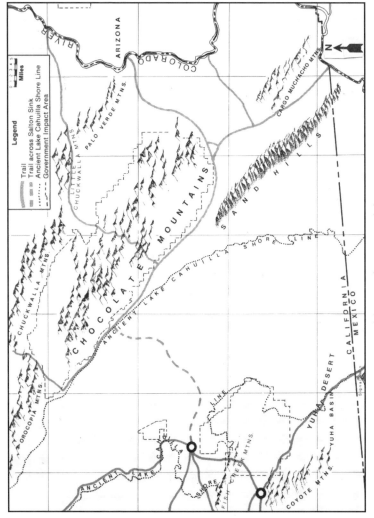

Trail System for Imperial County

tioned gathered on Hapaha Flat for their spring ceremony before returning to their permanent homes.

Where Agua Caliente Springs is today was the village of *Haawii* (water in rock). About three hundred years ago the *Haawii* people were driven from their village by a militant group who were thought to have come from the north, possibly northern Arizona. They were not *Kumeyaay* nor were they the warring Cocopa. The *Haawii* moved to the eastern edge of Vallecito Valley near the present day Vallecito County Park. Again the invaders kept raiding the *Haawii* who then finally merged with the *Amat Haapshuu* to the west of them.

The militant *Haakwapin*, as they came to be known, now had control of the village the *Haawii* had most recently vacated. It was from this point that the *Haakwapin* staged their raids on the peaceful desert villagers and also extended their activities up to the villages in the mountains. They always gave a warning—three smoke signals—of a coming raid. Young and old hid themselves and their belongings from the raiders. Finally, the combined desert and mountain *Kumeyaay* leaders met and decided the *Haakwapin* must be eliminated, and with their combined strength, they did just that. The men applied war paint on their faces and upper bodies. It was used for camouflage more than anything else.

The general term used to describe most of the people just mentioned is *Inyakiipaa*, people from the eastern mountain region to the desert. The trail system spread in all directions from the *Kwaaymii* homeland. To the north were the Julian people, the *Tulliipaa* (Mesa Grande and Santa Ysabel area), the *Hakwach* (Cupeño) around Warner Springs, and the Cahuilla. *Kwaaymii* went into Pine Valley and traded with the *Kwamaay*. Tom's mother was *Kwamaay* and these people went to Skye Valley for their temporary winter quarters. From Pine Valley the trail went through *Mataarawa'aa* country (Viejas Indian Reservation) and on to the coast from there. Essentially, all the *Kumeyaay* people traded with each other, from the coast to the Colorado River. They dealt with the Chemehuevi, Cahuilla and Cupeño to the north.

Uun'nyaw Kuupsaw—The Spirit of the Trail Guardian.

Wiitaawhiitl—the Trail Shrine.

19

Trail Shrines

At the top of Cottonwood Canyon is a granite outcrop which looks like an old, shawl-covered woman, watching over the trail to Mason Valley. The *Kwaaymii* call this *uun'nyaw kuupsaw*, the guardian of the trail, or more accurately, the Spirit of the Trail Guardian. About halfway down the canyon is the trail shrine. A huge white boulder along the trail marks the border of the sacred area. It was a custom to lay bay leaves on the marker when passing. The shrine can be seen directly below. It is a massive granite outcrop, perhaps 8 meters (25 ft.) high. Through time's erosion process this imposing rock has split apart, forming a natural cave. They called this cave *wiitaawhiitl*. A protruding ledge at its high northern entrance extends into the cavity forming the floor. It is on this ledge that travelers tossed thousands of small, rounded, granite stones in an appeal to the Trail Guardian for protection on their journey.

Along the trail is a difficult passage—a very steep, rocky section. The *Kwaaymii* carved a series of steps over this section which can still be seen today.

Hunting

Game was plentiful in the mountain and desert areas of the *Kwaaymii*. They hunted deer *(akwak)* with bow and arrow. They used just about every part of the animal for something— the brains in a tanning process to whiten the hide, the bones for awls and gaming pieces, the hoofs for ceremonial rattles, the entrails for making glue, tallow for treating chapped skin or lips and the hide for clothing and other uses. Women generally made the meat into jerky. They cut the meat in strips and cleaned off as much of the fat as possible, then laid the strips of meat over a large rock to dry in the sun, turning them periodically. If flies were a problem, they would put the meat in a basket and smoke it over a fire until it became very dry. If it looked like there was any fat on the meat after it was dried, they were very careful to scrape it all off to prevent the food from becoming rancid in storage. They cooked any fresh meat over an open fire.

The *Kwaaymii* hunted rabbits *(kwinyaw)* with a throwing stick or caught them with a net. They used the hides for clothing and blankets and cooked the meat in a pot of water with acorn flour added to make a stew. These people hunted Bighorn sheep in the mountains north of the Mason Valley area (their winter camping ground).

Before the flood in 1916, there was a lake at the east end of San Felipe Valley which had formed behind a natural dam in Sentenac Canyon. There was also a swamp which is now a lake in the Laguna Meadow area, and it was at these two places where the Indians hunted migrating ducks and geese. They caught these aquatic birds at night using a net. They cooked the meat in a stew or over a fire and saved the goose fat to mix with jimson weed leaves for medicinal purposes. They saved some bones to use in making jewelry.

Weapons, Tools and Fishing

The *Kwaaymii* made bows *(aatim)* from huckleberry branches, sometimes scrub oak. The illustration shows how they shaped the wood. It had to stay in this position for about two months. They took care to shade it so it would not dry too quickly. Otherwise it would crack and much valuable time could be lost during this initial process. After the wood dried, they worked it into the desired shape with a stone knife. Then

they smoothed the bow with an abrasive stone (much like sandpaper). Some bows were crudely made, others very finely made. As today, the product depended on the ability of the craftsman.

The bow string could be of sinew, fiber or twisted buckskin. The buckskin works well until it gets damp, then it has a tendency to stretch. The men usually carried several bow strings with them on a hunt. They cured the rawhide strings with tannic acid and twisted and treated the sinew with resin or fat.

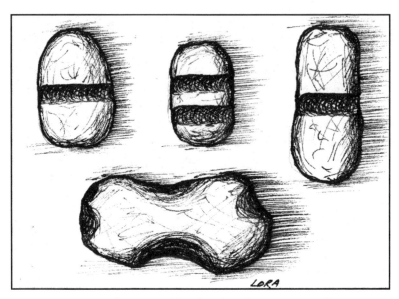

Arrow straighteners and hand ax found at *Kwaaymii* village.

The *Kwaaymii* made arrows *(paawii*—also the name for projectile points) from arrowweed. They cut the straightest stalks and stored them until dry. They straightened the arrow shafts on a small steatite stone with a carved groove bisecting the stone. The average size of an arrow straightener *(haapchuull)* was about 10 cm. (4 in.) long. They heated the stone then placed the arrow shaft in the groove to warp it until true. After they cut the shafts to the desired length and straightened them, they tied them in bundles and stored them until needed. The men kept only about twelve to eighteen arrows at ready. Men tested their arrows for accuracy by shooting them into a bank of soft dirt. If they were not quite right to the owner's satisfaction, he made adjustments—re-straightening and re-applying feathers. They used either three or four split feathers which had to be replaced after the arrow had been used several times. They wove an arrow sheath from milkweed or arrowweed fiber. The sheath, about 45 cm. (18 in.) long, held twelve to eighteen arrows, and was carried over the shoulder.

The first game killed by a young man on a regular hunt for the first time had to be given away. He could not eat any

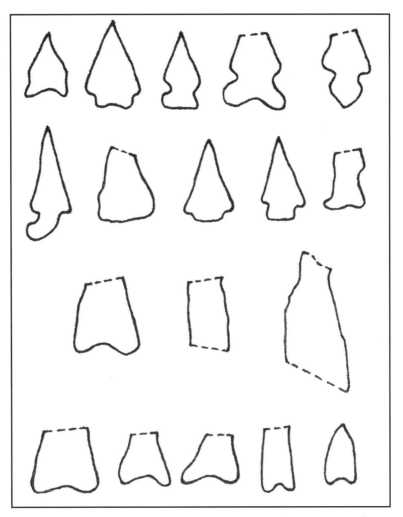

Shapes of projectile points from Lucas collection found at *Kwaaymii* village. Those in bottom row were fashioned from quartz.

of the meat but he shared it with everyone else. Children were never allowed in the areas where the men made their bows and arrows. These tools or weapons meant their survival and they could not take a chance that a young child might intrude and break or carry away something.

Men used a throwing stick for hunting rabbits. The wood they preferred to use was oak, wild lilac or chokecherry. They soaked and bent the stick, then when dried, they carved it flat with a stone knife. The *Kwaaymii* also used spears and small stone hatchets for weapons. It was not unusual for neighboring people to trade hunting areas so that all could share the variety of game. Some hunting trips lasted as long as a week, usually in the fall to prepare for the long winter months.

Although the *Kwaaymii* subsistence depended primarily on hunting and gathering, they did know about fishing. The older members of the village talked about the days when their ancestors fished in the desert (Lake Cahuilla was a fresh water lake which covered most of Imperial Valley, fed by the Colorado River). Tom says the men made nets from the cambium of arrowweed, which is very fine. "Two men would swim out with a log or in a canoe and drop the nets which were weighted with rocks, then pull them in. They used nets more than anything. However, they had some arrows with a crooked neck, with kind of a half-moon shoulder [point] on them. They had strings on them, and they could shoot the fish in shallow water. Along the ancient shore line [Lake Cahuilla] they made fish traps. When the waves were high the fish come in and they get caught in the traps."

Nets

The most common plant fibers used for making nets and ropes were mescal, or century plant, arrowweed and milkweed. The majority of these plants were found in the desert areas and the *Kwaaymii* usually made their nets in the winter months, preparing for summer in the mountains. They generally used arrowweed fiber to make nets for trapping rabbits, although on occasion they used nets of mescal fiber. They gathered arrowweed in the fall after it had reached its maturity.

Mescal was used to make heavier and larger nets for carrying large loads of perhaps fifty to one hundred pounds. Mescal nets were much stiffer than arrowweed nets, and were made with a supportive tumpline which was put around the forehead to suspend the net on the back. If the load was ex-

24

tremely heavy it was carried over the shoulder. Women could generally carry their own cookware, household items, personal things and a few blankets in a single net.

Milkweed, a popular fiber found in the mountains, was made into small carrying nets. The very finest of the fiber of this plant was woven into a cloth-like material and used for clothing. The dried leaves of the century plant were used to make rope. The leaves were pounded with a stick or small hand stone and the stringy fibers removed, then soaked in water and twisted together.

Scene of fall gathering area. *Drawing by SuSaan Garcia.*

Food Gathering and Preparation

Acorns *(kapash)* were gathered in the fall before the Kwaaymii began their long journey into the desert to their winter homes. Their gathering place was at the base of Sheephead Mountain in the Lagunas. The *Teshill, Kwatatl, Wiiapaayp* and *Kwaaymii* shared this area. Generally, only the women gathered the wild plants and seeds, but in harvesting the acorns the men and older children helped. Once the ripened acorns fell to the ground, it would not be long before the first snows would come to the mountains. Women put their babies in a type of cradleboard called the *hakwall* which they carried on their backs with straps over their shoulders. For very short, nearby gathering sessions, they preferred to use a small carrying net for the baby. But on more extended trips while they were busy gathering, they would hang the cradleboard in a nearby tree while they worked. The *hakwall* was made with either basket material or hide over a frame of huckleberry wood which was easy to bend into the desired shape. When they had finished gathering, the people visited briefly, sang their parting songs and celebrated with a thanksgiving ceremony in which they thanked the Great Spirit for the good harvest. Then they returned to their own villages to prepare for their winter migrations.

Each family kept acorns in a storage granary *(shakwiin)* which was a huge basket made by twisting and tying young willow branches together. The basket makers kept adding more branches until the baskets were thick and waterproof. A lid was made of the same material.

Bedrock mortar at fall gathering area.

26

Tom at age 5 standing by storage granaries used by his mother and grandmother. Aug. 24, 1908.

Acorns are ground into meal using a mortar or metate with a small hand stone. The meal is then swept into a very finely woven basket and washed several times to remove the tannic acid. When the water looks clear and tastes sweet, the meal is ready to use. From it they make soup, cakes and acorn mush *(saawii)* that is similar to a custard when cooled. They also mix the meal with a variety of ground foods or flour. What could not be carried by the *Kwaaymii* on the trip to the desert was stored in the granary for winter use. Quite often the granary itself was carried halfway down the mountain for easy access if additional meal was needed during the winter months. The mesquite bean is a favorite food found in the desert areas. When the beans are removed from the pod, they can be stored indefinitely and are taken out only as needed, roasted in a shallow pan, stirred until they become golden brown, then ground up. The meal has a sweet taste. Pinyon nuts are gathered and then roasted in a pit of hot coals. They are raked out and hit with a stick to remove the seed coverings. The seeds are roasted again in a shallow pan until they turn brown. Seeds are eaten whole or ground and mixed with grey sage or chia seeds. The grey sage seed is not only nourishing but is easy to gather. The seed pods are picked and laid on a flat rock to dry. The seeds are shaken out of the pods and then ground into flour. Even the stalk of this tender plant is edible and is succulent enough to be used as a substitute for water while traveling in the desert. Another nourishing food is the chia seed which is usually ground and made into soup. Chia or grey sage seeds are also mixed with ground pinyon nuts to make patties which are easy to carry when traveling. In the spring, these aborigines gathered fresh mustard greens, watercress and especially wild clover greens which were considered a delicacy.

Basketry

The *Kwaaymii* had many shapes, sizes and uses of baskets. Those used daily were not decorated much, but the women outdid each other when making baskets for their personal use.

SuSaan Kallich. Aug. 24, 1908.

Maria Alto at work making one of her beautiful baskets for which she was well known. c. 1922.

Quite often, feathers from woodpecker and mountain quail were woven into the basket for color and also attached to the basket when finished. Baskets used by shamans and chiefs were decorated with eagle feathers or pheasant feathers. The materials women favored for making baskets were deer grass and witch hazel. Deer grass was picked in the summer after it had reached its mature height and before it started to dry out. This grass can be bent without breaking and will not rot when it gets wet as some other grasses will. The stripped bark of witch hazel twigs was coiled around bunches of deer grass. Occasionally, baskets were made of tule, producing an attractive container of olive-green color, but were more fragile and did not last as long as the other ware.

They used bone awls for weaving basket materials in earlier days, but more recently used awls that they ground down from old files. Women kept awls of different sizes to work on various sized baskets. They kept an olla especially for soaking basket-making material overnight to keep it from drying out.

Maria Alto. c. 1916.

Maria Alto with unidentified children, Mt. Laguna, 1922. *Abbie Boutelle photo. Courtesy San Diego Museum of Man.*

Because they were very personal items, the *Kwaaymii* burned most of the decorated baskets at the owner's death or with the owner's image at the *Karuk* ceremonies. Consequently, there are not many around today. Coiled baskets were the typical style.

Pottery

The *Kwaaymii* made a variety of items from clay but the most common and useful was the olla *(saakaay)*. They made ollas in many shapes and sizes. The smallest was a bottle-shaped olla with a very small hole in it to feed infants whose mothers could not nurse (in which case they fed babies a mild, thin soup made from chia seed). Sometimes the women decorated these ollas. Generally, two main pots were used for cooking. One was used for acorn mush, the other for meat and greens. They used a carved stick for stirring and a saucer shaped olla, about the size of a cereal bowl, to dip the food

Pottery and baskets made by Tom's mother, Maria Alto.

out of the larger olla. A wood fire was built inside a ring of large rocks with an opening at one end to allow more fuel to be added. These large, wide-mouthed vessels were set on the rocks for cooking. *Kwaaymii* women usually cooked enough for their families to last two to three days. Cooking ware was not painted and the only decoration was an occasional incised design around the wide neck of the olla.

Smaller ollas were used for storing seeds, making tea, and for individual water jugs. They were usually decorated by either painting or incising (an older form of decoration). In modern times some of the small water jugs had double necks. Water storage ollas were extremely large, usually about 50 cm. (20 in.) or more in diameter. The water permeating the clay caused the olla to "sweat" and the evaporation kept the drinking water cool even in hot summer months. When the clay became too dry, the water jugs were then used for cooking if possible.

To make the pottery, large chunks of clay were broken up in a mortar, then ground to a fine powder on a flat grinding slab. The powder was brushed into a large, shallow clay pan (or similarly shaped basket) with a kind of whisk broom made from a clump of fresh pine needles. They hit the sides of the pan to get the small pebbles to the surface. Liquid from boiled cactus was mixed with the powder until the desired consistency was obtained. The cactus juice kept the clay from drying too fast while being worked. The damp clay was put in a sack and buried for a week or two, which made it more pliable and easier to work.

Small ollas were made in one day but larger ones took two. The clay was rolled between the palms of the hands to form long strips which were then rolled into a spiral to form the base of the olla. The sides were made by fitting one strip on top of another and at the same time working the inside with the hand, a smooth rock or a specially made clay tool, and the outside with the other hand or a wooden paddle. As soon as it was smoothed to the maker's satisfaction, the bottom half of the olla was set in the shade with something damp placed over it so that the exposed rim would not dry out. By the next day the clay of the half-finished olla was hardened sufficiently

SuSaan Kallich. c. 1910.

Women used clay and wood tools such as these to smooth the damp clay when making their ollas.

to hold the weight of the new clay as the maker formed the upper half, but with the rim remaining damp enough for the new clay to adhere to it. When the olla was finished it was placed in the shade until it looked dry. Then it was set out in the sun and turned often until it was completely dry and had a clear ring to it when tapped. Depending on the size of the olla, this pre-firing, drying process could take up to a week. Once the olla was dried it was ready to be decorated. Tom Lucas explains, "They use that black graphite to decorate the pottery. It's like a pencil lead. They work that up with a pine resin, then when the pot is baked [fired] it works right into the clay and it has a dark grey look. But that color won't show up too much if the pot is used for cooking because it smokes up. They decorated water-carrying pots with black all over and red oxide. The red oxide you usually get around the spring. They paint the pots before they fire them. If they paint that on real heavy it just bakes right into the pot.

"Some people make designs like triangles all the way around. Some were very elaborate—it just depended on the individual's own idea. Others had arrows on them. The most common design they used was the rattlesnake. I don't know why they do that—it shows the diamonds on there. They used that design very extensively on baskets too—not just our people, but a lot of others too. But it takes a very good craftsman to design a bird to look like a bird or an animal that looks like it's supposed to. They usually made stick animals with legs, heavy neck. The deer has been used quite a

36

SuSaan Kallich, Maria Alto, Tom Lucas—Laguna Indian Reservation. c. 1908.

bit too. You very seldom ever see any designs like a flower or something like that. Flowers don't show up very good. What shows up most is an animal or these zig-zag signs and rattlesnake signs. My mother decorated her pottery. I don't think I have any of those. She made her very best ones for people that wanted to buy them or for special people she gave them to. The women often times learn that [making and decorating pottery] from their mothers or from their own [women relatives], because an outsider won't teach another too much unless a girl is married into a family and they really like her—they'll show all they can to her. Otherwise it stays within their own [the girl's] family circle. Besides painting pottery, some of them would inscribe indentations in the clay after it was finished—before it was fired. That was an old, ancient way of decorating pots."

Only women made and decorated pottery. The usual color of the pottery in the mountain area is a reddish brown. There are three deposits of white clay (matahwaay) that Mr. Lucas knows of—near Campo, Warner Springs, and San Felipe Valley. The white clay was considered to be very precious. It makes up into very smooth, cream-colored pottery and requires nothing more than water as a mixing agent. It was prepared the same way as the local clay. The white clay was also used for paint.

During the summer months the Kwaaymii gathered dry oak bark which they used as fuel for firing their pottery. When they could get it by trading, they also used dry "buffalo chips" to add to the fire. It kept the fire burning hot and evenly. In recent times they used cow manure. They stored the bark and chips and covered them to protect them from getting wet. If any of this fuel was the slightest bit damp when burned, it created a cool spot which caused the pots to bake unevenly which weakened them. They never used pine because it smoked up the ollas.

The size of the fire pit was a little over a meter (4 ft.) deep and big enough to hold four medium-sized ollas. They covered the bottom of the pit with the oak bark and manure to a depth of about 20 cm. (8 in.). The ollas were placed in the pit and then completely surrounded and covered with the fuel.

The fire was usually started in the evening when the wind had died down, and it was allowed to burn without being disturbed until the ashes were entirely cold, which might take as long as two days. As soon as the pots were removed they were ready for use.

Mortars

Tom Lucas recalls the older *Kwaaymii* folks telling him there were not enough mortars to go around when the Indian population was at its peak. Considering the multitude of portable mortars and manos that adorn modem homes and the number of bedrock mortars still to be found in the area, the population in the Laguna Mountains could have been far higher than previous accounts have indicated. It is not uncommon to find mortars that have been worn completely through the rock from use.

Tom's grandmother, SuSaan Kallich, kneeling at her matate in front of a brush-covered ramada. She is wearing a gathering basket for a hat. Also shown is a winnowing basket, a throwing stick, and two bows by her right arm and a few of her ollas. c. 1912.

Although women usually had their own portable mortars and grinding slabs, they generally preferred to gather around larger bedrock mortars located in their immediate vicinity. It gave them a chance to visit while they worked. Most of the large mortars had a ramada built over them for protection from sun and wind. Four forked logs were anchored upright in the dirt with four more smaller logs fitted into the forks and attached with mescal rope to support a roof. Small branches were then secured on three sides of the structure for cross pieces to which brush or pine boughs were tied. The ramadas resembled houses but were not as sturdy.

There is a large mortar rock near the present house at the Lucas Ranch (formerly Laguna Indian Reservation), which Tom remembers his mother and grandmother using. The flat, smooth places on the rock were used to grind the acorns or seeds, and the holes were used to hold the grain and for grinding small seeds. To make the mortar holes, women chipped out the size hole they wanted, then used a large stone pestle which they turned in the hole to make it smooth. They added sand and water to speed the process. If the hole seemed to be off center, they chipped a little more out of it then continued working the hole to the preferred depth, which varied considerably.

Beverages

One of the most common beverages was tea made from the blossoms of the elderberry bush. It was considered to be very nourishing and was often given to women just before giving birth. The berries were also used which made a thick drink. A refreshing drink was tea made from wild mint leaves. A lot was made at one time and stored in ollas. It could be drunk several times a day, either hot or cold. The only alcoholic drink was made from the century plant. The young plants were roasted and had the consistency of a yam or sweet potato, but tasted much sweeter. The cooked plant was put in water and set in the sun to ferment. They didn't really use this much because they say, "It made you kind of goofy."

Tom's mother, Maria, grinding seeds. c. 1917.

Agriculture

The *Kwaaymii* didn't practice agriculture until about 1860.
At first, they cleared the fields near their villages by hand.
Soon they began to acquire a few iron tools and each year en-
larged the planting area. They irrigated the fields with water
from a nearby spring. They built an earth dam and let it fill
with water for several days, then opened the dam to allow the
water to flow into irrigation channels. After the government
set aside Indian lands, they issued the *Kwaaymii* one wagon,
one grindstone, one sickle and a few hand rakes. They were
promised more but received nothing.

About 1900 they planted an apple orchard. Sapsuckers
killed all but one tree, which is still living today. They also
grew a few pumpkins, the meat of which they dried in the
sun and stored for winter use. The agricultural period of these
people was short lived. By 1918, the year of the big influenza
epidemic, there were only two *Kwaaymii* remaining—Tom
Lucas and his mother, Maria Alto. Tom was fifteen years old.
His mother was nearing eighty.

Tom at age 15 in his first store-bought suit, 1918.

Agriculture was not a necessity with these people as it was with some other cultures. They had abundant varieties of food until the late 1800s when Indian land allotments were determined. The *Kwaaymii* (as well as other groups) were extremely limited in their traditional subsistence patterns by having to stay within their newly appropriated boundaries.

They were forced to try new innovations such as agriculture and raising cattle, but because of the lack of government support by way of "expert" know-how and needed tools and supplies, many had to search for jobs elsewhere to survive. Tom's mother and grandmother worked for local ranchers.

His mother subsequently became an expert horsewoman and learned enough about ranching to successfully raise her own cattle at the Laguna Reservation. During the fast-paced changes around the turn of the century, many Indians simply left their homelands to relocate at more remote reservations, trying to hold on to the only life they had known, or wanted to know.

Tom's mother, Maria, at Benton's Ranch in Corta Madera—c. 1910.

Maria Alto—1915.

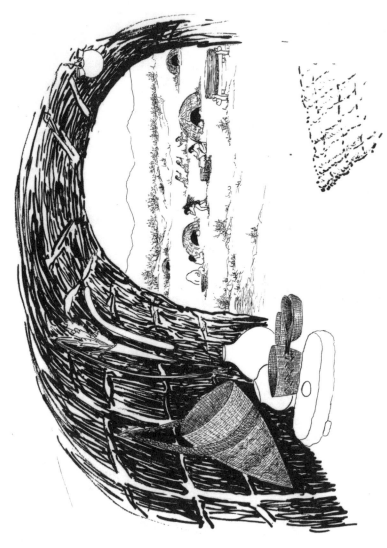

Artist's conception of Mason Valley Village. *Drawing by SuSaan Garcia.*

Chapter III

SOCIAL CUSTOMS

Clothing

THE ELEVATION OF THE LAGUNA MOUNTAIN area where the *Kwaaymii* lived is 5,500 to 6,000 feet. The weather extremes at that altitude required that they have a variety of suitable clothing. Women made all the clothing. They generally made summer clothing from woven milkweed fiber. The women peeled the outer layer from the stalk of the plant and shredded it to get the very fine fiber. Then they twisted the fibers together into a long cord for weaving. Women, and older girls who had gone through puberty rites, wore woven skirts and sometimes a woven shawl to cover their shoulders in the cooler summer evenings. They either went barefoot or wore sandals made of deer hide. As children do today, the *Kwaaymii* children preferred not to wear anything during summer days, but for short journeys and cool evenings they had a woven blanket and sandals to wear. Men and older boys wore breech cloths made of the woven milkweed fiber. They too had a small blanket to cover their shoulders if needed. In summer, men also wore sandals.

Deer, bear, and rabbit skins were used to make winter clothing. Bear skin blankets or wraps were much desired

47

but became very scarce within the last two hundred years. Sometimes skins were treated before they were tanned to retain the fur, which was worn next to the body for added warmth during extreme weather. Men wore long pants made of buckskin and usually buckskin moccasins which came to the knee. At their winter homes in the desert, if the weather permitted, they might wear sandals of thickly woven mescal fiber. Fur blankets covered the upper part of the body. In the early days, when bear were more abundant, they tanned and re-tanned the hides until they were extremely soft and pliable. They also used woven strips of rabbit fur and deer skin to make blankets. Young boys' winter clothing was fashioned after the men's. Women and girls wore knee-length moccasins with a skirt made of hide which covered the top of the moccasins, about mid-calf length. They also wore fur blankets to protect the upper part of their bodies. Babies were wrapped in woven rabbit skin blankets.

Tanning

Tanning skins was an exact and lengthy process. Women did the tanning except when they had a hide which was too large or heavy for them to handle by themselves. Then, the men helped with the process. Mr. Lucas explains, "They use the oak bark. It has tannic acid in it. They cook the bark and then they let the skin soak in it, usually for two days or until it's soaked through. If you leave it in too long it might rot the skin. Then they take the skin out and work it over a wood chisel, which is a log put into the ground with the end cut at an angle. To store skins with the hair on them until ready to use, they would treat the fur side with salt water. That kept the mites and small bugs out of the fur. Then they would take it out and soak it again, let it half dry and scrape the under side off down to the actual hide. If they wanted to take the hair off, they would put the hide in a big pot of ash. The ash makes the skin soft and they take a scraper made out of deer ribs or some kind of bone—but not a knife because it's too sharp and would cut the hide. They put the hide over the chisel and work on the hide that way, scraping.

"If they wanted the deer skin white, they would take the brain of the deer and cook that. In the process, it turns into something like a lard. They mix that with good, clean ashes. Then they take that and work it into the hide, then they turn it over and put it on the other side of the hide. They tie the hide up in a tree and put heavy weights on it to stretch it down and then they twist the hide back and forth. That's the way that lard works into the hide. On hard to reach areas, you work that by hand. Then they take it down and work it over the wood chisel—back and forth. It has to be wood—a rock would cut the hide. After being worked for awhile, it turns real white. It's pretty thin but it's really soft and it's snow white. They used that for women's skirts."

Hair

The adults and children wore their hair long. The men's hair was about shoulder length and was generally tied at the back of the neck. The women wore their hair longer and usually braided and tied it at each side of the head, so that it covered their ears. In early times almost everyone wore bangs. The hair was cut with a stone or obsidian knife. The only time a woman had short hair was when it was cut off during the time of mourning. If it was the woman's husband who died, she usually waited about two years before remarrying—long enough for her hair to grow out again. The hair was combed with forked manzanita sticks or carved bones. They wore headbands made of braided or woven fiber and buckskin. Each was decorated to the wearer's taste but many used feathers.

Hair trimmings (with the exception of the hair cut off by mourners that was saved for the *Karuk* ceremony) and nail trimmings were carefully disposed of to keep evil witches or medicine men from using them in spells against the reluctant donor. Hats were worn by women but they were nothing more than small gathering baskets used to gather herbs or berries. In later days, regular straw hats were worn.

49

Jewelry

It was mostly the women who wore jewelry. It would have been in the way of the average man while running or hunting. The men who did wear jewelry were usually medicine men or very old. They made necklaces with small bird bones, painted or dyed berries, and wild cherry nuts. The bones were cut with an obsidian knife and sanded down until they were very smooth. Most of the berries were painted red or black, or occasionally dyed yellow with the root of the wild celery plant. Earrings were usually made with seashells, hard wood, or small, brightly colored pebbles. Some gold and silver was used but they were afraid to display it after the coming of the Spanish. Ear piercing was done with a bone, probably a deer bone that had been cracked and worked until the sides were smooth and the point very sharp. The ear lobe was pinched first then pierced. A small greased fiber was inserted into the hole and left there until the ear healed.

Tattoos

To the *Kwaaymii,* tattooing oneself was hardly more than a fad, although they did practice it. They recognized that to other tribes, such as the Yuma people, it meant a sign of their ancestry or clan affiliation. When the *Kwaaymii* did use tattooing, it generally consisted of lines marked on the face. The only known instance of using an animal figure was on the arm of a local snake charmer. Anyone could do the tattooing. They used a fine bone needle and the juice of the wild chokecherry plant. Both men and women were known to display tattoos.

Social Dances

There were dances that were held occasionally just for an excuse to socialize or to celebrate an exceptionally successful hunt or possibly a "coming out party" for the young women who had just gone through the annual puberty rite ceremony. Sometimes these dances started during the day and continued into the night. They broke up as people became tired and started going home. The three dances Mr. Lucas can recall are the *orap, namii,* and *tomann.* All three dances were known by all the groups (the mountain, coastal and desert peoples).

They built a large ramada (dance house) and danced in a circle around a fire. The dancers started counterclockwise, then the people at the tail became the leaders as they turned and danced in the opposite direction. They danced in pairs —either two men, two women, or a man and his wife—and moved forward in step with rattles or drums. Children were not usually permitted at social dances. These social dances were very cheerful and the "grown-ups" came to relax and have a good time.

Musical Instruments

The flute, called *haaluu,* was made from either mountain bamboo or the desert reeds. They hollowed it out by using a small stick that they heated in a fire and worked back and forth. They drilled four holes in the hollow tube. The end had to be covered with the finger of one hand while it was being played. This was used for entertainment purposes only.

Rattles were the most common instruments. They were used for ceremonials and for social dances. The head shaman used a rattle made from deer hoofs. Each hoof was dried and tied to a separate thin fiber cord about 30 cm. (1 ft.) long. There were as many as two dozen hoofs tied together on a handle for one rattle. It makes a soft, muted, hollow sound as the hoofs hit against each other.

Three other types of rattles were used by the *Kwaaymii* for either dances or ceremonies. One was made of deer hide. It was fashioned by pouring hot sand into a piece of wet deer hide. The edges were bunched together and tied at the top and allowed to dry, which took about ten days. Once dried, the sand was poured out, small pebbles put in its place and a handle was attached with wet deer hide thongs. The rough edges of the rounded hide were neatly trimmed. These rattles were usually decorated by painting them or adding feathers, or both.

51

Another type was made from wild gourds found in the mountain and high desert areas. A hole was drilled in the gourd just big enough for a handle to be wedged in. They put in small pebbles and attached the handle by wet deer hide straps wrapped around the gourd to hold the handle securely in place. These were also painted or had feathers attached for decoration. The third kind was a finger rattle made of clay. Small rocks were put into the bulb while it was being formed, and a ring was made at one end. These could be painted and were fired with other pottery. To keep the bulb from shattering while being fired, a twig was used to make a hole in the bulb. This type of rattle was rarely used because of its fragile quality.

Drums were used only for social dances. They were too loud to use at ceremonial gatherings. Hollow logs were used and the ends were smoothed symmetrically. The inside was cleaned out by burning and scraping with a knife. The ends were covered with hide, preferably deerskin, and then decorated by painting or by imbedding small, colorful stones into the wood. Feathers were also employed. Each decorated instrument was unique. Colorful feathers were used more than anything else for decorative purposes. Attaching feathers was less time-consuming than artful painting.

Toys

Cattails were gathered for children to play with. They were colored with a red dye from berries, a yellow dye made from the giant celery plants that are found along creeks throughout the area, and brown dye from the tannic acid of the oak. These were fashioned into dolls by inserting small twigs to represent arms and legs, and occasionally corn silk was added for hair. The cattails were then treated with pine resin to keep them from drying out and blowing away. Children fashioned little dolls and animals from clay that was left over from what was being used at the time by their mothers. Boys made their own bows and arrows. They would mimic adult counterparts in their play.

Games

These mountain people had little time to spend in idle amusement, but occasionally some of the men would gather to play *apall,* a very old and popular stick game. Four playing pieces are used in *apall.* Two sticks about 10 cm. (4 in.) long and 1.5 cm. (0.6 in.) wide are cut from a branch of the elderberry bush. Each stick is then halved lengthwise. The players divide themselves into two groups. One group wagers on the flat side of the sticks, the other on the rounded side. One player tosses the sticks into the air. If he is in the group betting on the "flats" then the sticks that fall with the flat side up are worth more than the sticks that fall with the rounded side up, and vice versa. Venison jerky and other items of food were common wagers.

In a similar game, a single playing piece was used. It was made from a section cut out of a large animal leg bone, with both ends cut flat. One player tosses the piece into the air and he wins only if it lands on one of the flat ends.

The *Kwaaymii* had a ball game resembling soccer that was played between tribes. It required considerable skill and endurance. The playing field extended the entire length of the valley now covered by Cuyamaca Reservoir, about 3 km. (2 mi.). The ball was made from the root of the wild honeysuckle plant. This plant forms a gnarled bulb of very hard wood just below ground level. One of these roots was carefully selected. The root extensions and stalks were trimmed off and the bulb was shaped into a sphere against a rough rock, then smoothed against a finer grained rock. The finished ball was about 15 cm. (6 in.) in diameter.

53

The opposing teams, each with two men, played barefoot. One player from each team began the game by racing to the ball previously placed in the center of the valley and trying to "kick" the ball toward the opposing goal (a player slipped his toes under the ball and lifted and flipped it with a kicking motion). The second man of the team was already stationed closer to the goal he was defending in order to intercept the ball. Sometimes one player would allow the opposing player to run for awhile with the ball, then would catch up to him and try to take it back. Istaako, a great uncle of Tom Lucas, played this game extremely well. He was small and wiry and very fast. Once he got the ball, "...it was goodbye ball—he's gonna make it home." A variation of this game was played with four men to a side, using clubs to maneuver the ball toward the goal.

Animals and Pets

The only domesticated animal the *Kwaaymii* had until recent times was the dog. Most dogs were trained for hunting. A dog could track a wounded animal, tree squirrels, or otherwise assist in the hunt. Some were used for watch dogs against an intruding enemy. After the Spanish arrived, many Indians started raising stock animals. The *Kwaaymii* kept mostly cattle and horses. They have a legend that horses had been here long before the Spanish, but no one had thought to use them for anything. Halters for horses were made out of horse hair or buckskin. Blankets were made of woven milkweed, willow fiber, horse hair, or deer skin that was shaped while wet to the horse's back. Fiber blankets were preferred. They tried raising pigs but Tom says they got into everything and "...that most Indians don't like them because they look entirely too much like human beings. They said that they were human beings at one time and they've been condemned...[creation myth]."

The eagle *(kwaaypaay)* is "...the leader of men, then birds... It's been with the people since the beginning of people and it's been with the people and the animals and birds. My mother's grandfather was very slender and a good climber. They used to let him go after the baby eagles. They usually had two. He let his toenails grow long so he could scale the cliffs. They had rope and nets. He'd tie the nets and rope around himself. If he could, he would go to the top and let the babies down in the net from the top. That's the easiest way. They take the babies home and keep them in a cage, sometimes for a year. They make the cage out of reeds and wood. They stick the big sticks into the ground. They make holes in the cage where they put food and water. Someone has to hunt every day to feed them—mostly rabbit. Sometimes they would hang the cage pretty far off the ground so animals wouldn't bother it."

Although young eagles were caught and cared for, they were kept only for feathers and sacrificial purposes (see section on the *Karuk*). Occasionally young birds were picked up and kept as pets until able to fly, then were released. Domestic cats were unheard of until recent times. Tom had several pets when he was a boy. He caught rabbits, raccoons and various kinds of birds which he raised and cared for until they were able to fend for themselves.

Chapter IV

POLITICAL ORGANIZATION

Village Leaders, Chiefs and Shamans

EACH VILLAGE HAD ITS own council. One man's judgment was
not sufficient to decide an issue. It was the council's responsibility to decide what was best and to discuss all matters relative to the welfare of everyone in the village. The size of the
council depended entirely on the size of the village. It consisted of chief *(kwaaypaay)*, shaman *(kwisiiyaay*—either male
or female) and older members of the village who were well
thought of, fair in judgment, and competent. Members were
not appointed but were just asked to sit in. If someone was
brought before the council on criminal or civil charges and
was related to one of the members, then that member would
step down and not decide on that issue. All grievances were
taken to the council but in addition were sometimes handled
with revenge.

In the event of a murder, the *Kwaaymii* philosophy was
"an eye for an eye." The guilty paid with his life. The council
might decide to push him over a cliff or the shaman would
dispatch him with a poisonous concoction. There was one
instance when a young man went a little "crazy." He would
shoot the water jugs the women were carrying from the

spring and shoot at children just to watch them scatter. They found two or three people dead, and this man, who was suspected of killing them, turned up with items that belonged to the deceased. Then a miner and a sheepherder disappeared. Everyone was afraid he might kill an influential rancher or Mexican official which might mean a retaliation that would wipe out the village. The council decided his fate and the entire village was in on the plot. Everyone kept telling him he looked sick and that he should go see the medicine man. After a few days, he believed he was sick and went to the medicine man who gave him something to drink. He simply went to sleep and never woke up. Survival of the whole group had top priority.

The punishment for stealing was a public flogging with a hard mescal fiber rope. Everyone had to be there, even if they did not actually watch. There was never any blame put on the spouse of an accused or guilty person.

When a chief died, his son took over. In the event there was no son, a younger brother might take his place. This was the case with the last *Kwaaymii* chief, Valentine, and his brother, Juan Baptiste. They were originally named *Parahaan* and *Parakann* (or *Saatiiko*), after the legend ("Old Woman's Twins"—see Chapter VI) but were baptized in the Catholic Church as Valentine and Juan Baptiste. At the chief's death, his headdress and other items symbolic of his position were passed on to his successor, with the exception of personal amulets. All mundane items were either broken or burned and buried with the owner's remains.

Potential chiefs, shamans and village leaders were picked from the young men just completing the puberty rites. The shamans picked only the ones who showed promise for further esoteric instruction and development. A very small village of three or four families might not have a chief, but at least it had a leader of some kind—a shaman or village elder.

The last *Kwaaymii* shaman, *Parakann* (Juan Baptiste), was married to a Cupeño Indian woman they called Old Lady Gertrude. *Parakann* was a snake charmer. Tom witnessed him take complete control over a large rattlesnake. He was well known for his snake medicine and was often called to dis-

Valentine, the last *Kwaaymii* chief. c. 1880.

tant villages to help. His wife was well known for her herbal medicine. She was also considered a shaman.

There were many varying degrees of shamanism, but it was the head shaman who was acutely aware of the esoteric aspect of his profession. The last really powerful medicine man who lived with the *Kwaaymii* was Yellow Sky. His Indian name was *Amaay Kwakwas*. His father was *Kwaaymii* and his mother was *Kwichaan Awik* (Yuma). In this particular instance the father had chosen to live with his wife's people, and Yellow Sky was born a *Kwichaan Awik*, learning his trade there. He never married, and when his mother and father died, he asked to live with the *Kwaaymii* for the remainder of his years. He was more than welcomed. Besides his usefulness as a great shaman and healer, he was always eager to help people with their chores.

Cases have been known in which a woman took over, acting as "chief." They called her *kwachukwaataay*, which means "command." She would have been a wiser, older woman who was probably known as a shaman in her own right.

During the last visit of Halley's Comet, all the leaders of the tribes got together and went through several nights in trance (sometimes induced by jimson weed). The premonition that came out of that meeting was, "...they saw many people dying, many, many miles away, across the big water..." What they foretold was World War I. Many young men volunteered to fight in that war although they were not yet considered United States citizens (citizenship for American Indians came in 1924). The leaders also had told of the coming of the Spanish, "...they shall come forth, men on the horses, wear shiny jacket. They will lay waste—plunder."

Generally speaking, the chief was head of the village and council. The shaman was depended upon heavily for his guidance and inner visions and wisdom. They both had charms or talismans of clay which they used during meditation. They say some could pick up one of those charms and know what the owner had been thinking. It was believed that if a shaman misused his gift he would end up being a cripple, or some major mishap would ruin his life.

If a shaman was called to a house to heal a sick person, before going he would meditate all night and would know what to do the next morning. "Once a kid fell and busted in his skull. The bone was caved in…Someone went and got some eggs from down in the lowlands. She [Old Lady Gertrude] made a paste out of the eggs and pine resin and shaved the hair good and put the paste on that spot. When it dried up it pulled up the bones good as new. That kid grew up as if nothing happened. It has to be a natural gifted person, and when they see that, they help them to develop it. You just can't give them the power, but they can guide them spiritually."

Chapter V

THE LIFE CYCLE

Birth

WHEN IT CAME TIME for a baby to be born, the mother stayed at home or went to her mother's house, whichever was the most comfortable place for the mother-to-be. They sent for a birth attendant—usually an elderly woman who was well known for that—even if they had to go out of the village to find her. She was known as *hakwall kupshaw,* the tender of the young. If the old woman was really good she could tell exactly what was happening—the condition of mother and baby, when to cut the umbilical cord, and so forth—even at night with no light. When the baby was born, the old woman held it and said a prayer over it relating to the creation that had given it life. She buried the afterbirth, but it is not known if there was a particular ritual involved.

Before the baby was born, the mother was often given elderberry tea, which was very nourishing and relaxing. After the baby was born, the husband was not allowed to see mother or baby until everything was safe, usually one to two days. There was no curiosity attached to the event—it was a natural occurrence. Only very close relatives came by to see the new arrival. They were careful not to expose the infant to crowds too soon because they felt that there was the possibility that a "wrong spiritual influence" could take over the child. He had to be protected both physically and spiritually until he was strong enough to be on his own—usually about two months.

There were no taboos concerning the resuming of sexual relations between the parents. The woman had to feel strong and back to normal. The average number of children in a family was two to four, rarely more. There was a high infant mortality rate. Twins were considered abundant blessings. Deformities were rare—usually considered to be a result of incestuous marriage of too closely related cousins. First and second cousin marriages were neither approved of nor desired.

If a new mother was not able to breast feed her baby they made a thin soup from ground chia seed (sometimes mixed with acorn flour) and fed that to the infant from a very small olla with a reed straw. Occasionally other women who were breast feeding would be sought after to help feed the infant.

Usually babies were about two months old before they were given a name. Again the "wrong spiritual influence" might be able to do harm if the child's name was known. As an adult, a person might earn a new name like the man who was out hunting and was mauled by a bear. His friends rescued him and killed the bear. After that incident the man was called *Namuuleporwur*, the one the bear could not out-do.

Babies were carried in cradleboards of woven reeds with a feathered shade across the top. Occasionally they were made with a huckleberry frame and were covered with hide. Very small babies were more often carried in nets. The beds were made of woven basket material and were lined with a rabbit skin mattress which was made by twisting tanned strips of rabbit fur around a fiber rope, keeping the fur to the outside, then weaving the twisted strips. Cooked deer marrow was applied to the hide to waterproof it. Woven rabbit fur blankets were also made for winter use.

The word *hakwall* (young) is used many ways and has to be understood in context. The cradleboard is referred to as *hakwall*, the old woman who helps at birth is called *hakwall kupshaw* and the baby's blanket is *hakwall,* or sometimes called *hakwall chaapit* (baby cover).

If a child was orphaned, the closest woman relative took him over. If the woman was a widow and had nothing, then the village elders decided who should care for that child (or children). Sometimes they were perfect strangers but always the best was done to give a child every chance. If a child's father died, the mother would do the best she could, but more often than not would move in with her parents. A man left alone with a child usually sought help from either his or his wife's female relatives. It didn't matter which—whoever was capable of taking on the responsibility. Sometimes in the case of a divorce, the children were divided between the parents, simply as a matter of economy.

To quote Mr. Lucas, "We exchange gifts quite often. But we didn't celebrate birthdays or things like that. If a child lost all his relatives—well—at the end of the year [fall, *saa'ii* time] or whenever they can give, they do give some gifts, things that will be helpful to him. They give things like a woven blanket or some moccasins. Others just take pity on him and show him how to make things. That was supposed to be the very best gift you could give to a child."

The care and welfare of children were of utmost importance to these people.

Puberty Rites

Boys—The *Taakaayp* ceremony for boys was held annually. All boys received three days of instruction from the chief, head shaman and guardians (the gifted men or lesser shamans). The nature of the instruction was spiritual, political, economic and social—virtually every aspect of *Kwaaymii* society. Naturally, young boys received some of this at home from fathers or uncles, but this particular ceremony was to impress upon older boys the importance of becoming responsible adults.

The boys who were to go through the ceremony were gathered together in one place—a specially built sweathouse.

Tom at age 13.

They stayed there for the entire three days and were not allowed contact with anyone else in the village. They fasted the entire time and were to be careful of what they thought or said about anyone. They were to concentrate on the seriousness of their instruction. Toward the end of the three-day period, the boys lay on a mat of steaming bitter grass that had been piled up over a pit of burning coals. While they lay on this they sang a one word chant. This was a spiritual purification, and the head shaman watched closely. After that they were given a swallow of tea made from jimson weed root and then were told to sleep. Again, the adults watched the boys carefully. The guardians and shaman each put a hand on the boys' heads and said some special words. As each one came out from under the influence of the drink, he was questioned as to what he experienced. For those boys who had nothing to tell, the *Taakaayp* was over. The ones who the shaman felt had meaningful inner experiences were given further religious instruction over a period of time. These were the ones who would become the leaders or the varying degrees of gifted men or even the chief (although this position was usually passed from father to son). The *Kwaaymii* relied heavily on these men (and occasionally women) for their prophecies and healing abilities.

After the initial ceremony, the boys were allowed to eat a little food, but not any fats until they felt "normal" again. Bayberry leaves were put in a big pot of hot water and the boys sat over that with a blanket covering them to sweat out all the "poisons." Then they were given a massage. The *Taakaayp* ceremony had been discontinued by the late 1800s. But Tom's father and grandfather went through it, as well as all the other men who were still living in the *Kwaaymii* village during Tom's childhood.

Girls—*Taakaayp,* roughly translated, means quietly settling down. This ceremony for the girls was also held annually. The girls were taken to a special hut made for this purpose called the *awaa taakaayp* (the house of settling down). The girls fasted for three days and were instructed by older women in the village as to what was expected of them as good mothers, homemakers and respected members of the village.

Part of the girls' ceremony was religious but was not as intense as the boys'. Girls also lay on the steaming grass mats. They were ritually bathed and dressed in new clothing and their faces were covered. They were then taken together to be presented to the village where their face coverings were removed so people could see they were "new" people—girls that had become young women. Villagers offered them food and celebrated with singing. The chief asked for protection and guidance for them.

Marriage

A young man would watch the young woman he was interested in for a long time to make sure she was healthy and able to do the things required to take care of a house and family. At the same time, the young man had to prove himself as a hunter and provider and capable of handling a family. Once the man had decided on his mate, he went to her parents. He paid a "bride price"—something to make the agreement binding—to the young woman's parents. If he couldn't afford a horse, then he must give the best that he had. A good hunter might bring his prospective parents-in-law a whole deer. This gesture was to show respect for his in-laws, that he was aware that they had created the woman that would be his other half.

When the agreement was made, friends and family brought food and gathered at the dance house (usually just a large ramada) in the man's village. They took the young couple before the chief and he would tell them, "Now the two of you are united; you're on your own." Then to the people he would say, "This girl is no longer alone. She is a married woman now and the husband is no longer single. He has to take care of what he has. If you can help him, then help him."

Before the marriage took place, the man usually built a house for them near his own family. But there were sometimes extenuating circumstances which might alter the norm. If the girl's mother was a widow and alone, the couple could either move in with her, or the young man might build a new

Tom—July 20, 1926.

house for the three of them. If they were married before he built their house, they could live with his parents until the house was built. Occasionally the parents of a young man, who was bashful but would otherwise make a good provider, might arrange a marriage with the girl's parents. There was no period of courtship, but the girls always knew who was considering them for a wife. The interest was mutual. A girl might let the young man know by smiling at him, but she never made any obvious gestures or advances.

Most young men married in their early twenties. The women married a little younger. The young men weren't allowed to go on the men's hunting trips until they were in their twenties and seemed capable. Having "good looks" was not a consideration in picking a marriage partner. "Good looks didn't bring on good blankets. It was the capability of a man [or woman] that counted." *Kwaaymii* people usually married within their village, sub-tribe or tribe, but they were careful to be sure they were not too closely related. Anything closer than third cousins was strictly taboo. They believed an incestuous marriage produced half-wit offspring or brought on premature blindness in their children.

Divorce

"If things didn't go just right, and it happens—no one's perfect—if a man just isn't any good, he might decide to go over the hill and find another woman to live with. He can't support two or three and his regular wife goes hungry and his kids go hungry. Something's got to be done. But she belongs to him. They can't part blinded. It has to be taken up with the chief or the headman and they tell him it's either do right or that's it. In that case the wife gets to keep all the possessions, the house and everything they own. But if she is no good then it's just the other way around—they order her out. That's just the way it is.

"After a man has been married he's on his own, goes wherever he wants. After a divorce he has to build another house for himself. But after a divorce the woman can go back

The cabin which was built by Tom for his family in 1923. It is located just a few yards from where his mother's house once stood.

Harvesting wheat at the reservation, 1932.

Tom building the fireplace at the cabin, 1931.

to her parents. There's one thing about Indians—they will not kick their daughter in the face—never—no matter what happened to her, whether it was her fault or not. If it was not her fault, they take really good care of her and do everything possible to rehabilitate her and they hope in time she will find someone who is better for her, and they often do. They don't go much by looks and all that, it's the idea of a home and to bring forth comfort and peace and quiet and that's the way it ought to be. Sometimes when there are children they divide them if the man likes them well enough—sometimes the woman takes them all, but it's awful hard to feed and care for them alone unless she has relatives that will help to support them. That's why they always tell them to think things over— that the woman was the starlight of your eyes, the very tune of the song in your heart. Now, think that over. They [the chief or elders] give them a chance, but if it still don't work then it's no use to go on. As a rule, most all of them are attached to their children."

Death

The Elderly—The older members of the villages were always looked up to and respected for their years of accumulated knowledge. Under no circumstances were children allowed to make fun of an old person for any reason. The old ones were proud of their wrinkles and grey hair (if any) —they earned them with plenty of hard work. The cunning and wisdom that had kept them alive for so long earned them respect.

"Old" to the *Kwaaymii* was about eighty years and older. It wasn't unusual to find people who had lived a century or more. Tom's grandmother lived to be about one hundred fifteen years old. In the last two or three generations most births were recorded in the church then transferred to county records. But previously, ages were calculated by an event which took place near the time of a baby's birth. Surprisingly, their calculations were fairly accurate. Tom Lucas was born in the winter *(hiichur* or *saa'ii)* during one of the biggest snowstorms

Maria Alto—1880.

SuSaan Kallich

(tomus) they had seen in years. His recorded birth date is 20 February 1903.

Even though they were past their years of productivity, the older folks were consulted on important matters in village and tribal affairs. The old men spent a good deal of time in the sweathouse which served not only as a meeting place but also for secret religious ceremonies (Mr. Lucas couldn't elaborate on the secret ceremonies—the custom of using the sweathouse had been discontinued by the early twentieth century).

Maria Alto—1916.

The sweathouse was not just a "senior citizen" social gathering place but was used for religious purification—clearing oneself out in preparation for making important decisions —or even preparing oneself for death. "It is said that the old people talked of the *saa'ii*, the buzzard that fans his wings and keeps the warmth of the fire from them. *Saa'ii* time is winter, when everything is dead, cold—no growth."

Pipe made by Tom Lucas. Tom found the steatite pipe bowl at the old *Kwaaymii* village site.

The men smoked pipes usually made with a carved soapstone (steatite) bowl and a reed stem. Occasionally they used clay bowls. They decorated pipes with inlaid shells and rocks or carved designs and then they attached feathers or beads. Eagle and pheasant feathers were for chiefs and shamans only. They smoked a tobacco that grows in the desert foothills called *haatipaa op* ("coyote tobacco"). It is very mild, similar to Bull Durham. Only older people smoked when they did not have to run or do any more heavy work. The old women sometimes smoked too, but they usually gathered at a friend's house. On very *rare* occasions, a highly respected, old medicine woman might be invited to join the men in the sweathouse.

Construction of the sweathouse was simple. Framing pine or juniper log ends were set into the ground about 30 cm. (1 ft.) in a ring leaning in toward the center. They were tied together near the top and smaller branches were attached for cross pieces to support a mud and straw covering. When finished, the sweathouse resembled a mud igloo with a small crawl hole at the base and a small smoke hole at the top. It was large enough for about a dozen people to sit inside around the fire. Children were warned to stay away because "...the old spirits will get you."

Cremation—When someone died the relatives sent out word to other more distant relatives and friends. By early evening, the day of the death, there might be a dozen or more people around the body, chanting their laments and praises of the dead person. If it was someone who had been well thought of by all (including other tribes), or a good leader or shaman, there might have been well over a hundred people gathered by late night.

The songs and chants continued until just before dawn when the body was prepared for cremation. They believed if the spirit left the body with the rising sun, it was able to get off to a fresh start on its new adventure.

The Indians practiced cremation until 1860, when the priests banned the practice, calling it "sacrilegious." The missionary influence had been at work for nearly a century and was slowly absorbing the aboriginal culture. There were a few remote groups that continued secretly with the cremation practice for a number of years. But the Church by then had already instilled the "fear of God" into these natives. The practice of burning bodies *and* their possessions was sinful and meant sure punishment from God and/or the Church—"... your last chance for salvation. Give your body and your possessions to God. . ." (via the Church).

The Indian's idea of burning the personal possessions of the deceased is easy enough to understand because of their belief in the hereafter. Naturally it would be more pleasant for the spirit to have the things with it in its new life that it had enjoyed in its earthly life, i.e., bow and arrows, a favorite basket, and so forth.

As mentioned, the cremation took place at dawn. At this time usually only a very personal item of the deceased was burned with the body. Other things were saved for the *Karuk* ceremony which would take place about a year later. The body was laid on pine logs and branches and was allowed to burn untouched until cremation was complete. When the ashes had completely cooled, they were scraped up and put in a large olla, then buried. The old cremation and burial sites of the *Kwaaymii* were located near the *Kwaaymii* village just behind a small hill. The newer burial ground that has been in use since 1860 is situated on a hill overlooking the meadow east of the largest of the old *Kwaaymii* villages, *Iiahkaay*.

When a person died, the closest woman relative cut her hair extremely short with a stone knife. The cut hair was put into an olla, which was then hidden or tied up in a tree located on the trail near the cremation site. There were many stories of spirits being seen or heard along that trail. The hair was used later in making doll images of the deceased for the *Karuk* ceremony.

Women relatives (and friends) often painted their faces to indicate to others their state of mourning. The most common form of facial decoration was three or four horizontal streaks across each cheek. They used either black graphite or ashes mixed with goose fat. Occasionally women covered their faces with white clay paint called *matahwaay* (white earth) before adding the black streaks. "It would take many tears to wash away the black."

The Karuk—Probably, the most impressive ceremony the *Kwaaymii* practiced was the *Karuk*, the mourning ceremony which assured proper departure of the spirits to the hereafter.

These aboriginal people had a strong belief in the hereafter and they prepared for it during the course of their lives. They believed after a person died, his spirit stayed around for about a year, assimilating its life's lessons and experiences. Then during the *Karuk*, when it was time for the spirit to move on, it was met on "the bridge between the two worlds" by a spirit guide. If the person had been good in his life, his spirit was guided over the bridge. If bad, the spirit was left on the path to find its own way over the bridge—a very doubtful accomplishment. Shamans could perceive this process in their visions.

The *Karuk* ceremony. *Drawing by SuSaan Garcia.*

The last *Karuk* ceremony was held at the *Wiiapaayp* area on 25 August 1908. The *Wiiapaayp* (known today as Cuyapaipe Reservation) was used for this last joint *Karuk* ceremony because of its large, accessible areas which could accommodate many visitors. Many of the other villages were located in remote wooded areas, and many had been reduced in population to where there was but a single family remaining.

The population decrease and economic condition of many native groups in the late 1800s and early 1900s dictated that they band together if they wished to continue traditional cultural habits. However, it was not necessarily an uncommon practice for them to join together in the earlier days for major social or religious events. Tom recalls his grandmother relating a time in the early 1800s when the three *Kwaaymii* villages (*Wiihanuul, Kwaaymii* and *liahkaay)* hosted the *Karuk,* as well as many other ceremonies and celebrations.

The late summer *Karuk* ceremony was for those who had died within the previous year. If a person had died only a few months before the ceremony was to take place, the relatives

81

waited for the next year's ceremony. A few months was not enough time for the spirit to remember all its experiences nor was it a long enough time for proper mourning.

When it came time for the *Karuk*, other villages and tribes were invited. Some traveled as far as 150 miles to attend. They would be the ones who would be given valuable items that had belonged to the deceased—things that had been put aside expressly for this purpose—such as a good rabbit skin blanket. Nearby friends or relatives were not given any possessions because the items could not be seen again by the deceased's family. Although the *Kwaaymii* burned personal possessions, they did not simply destroy everything. Good blankets or work baskets—whatever might be useful to someone in need—were given to distant friends or relatives.

About two days before the ceremony, relatives started making images of the departed spirits. The images were constructed from reeds which had been gathered in the desert area. The reeds averaged a little over a meter (3-4 ft.) long and the images were about the same length. Occasionally they were much smaller, depending on the individual's ability to obtain enough materials. New clothing was made for the images. The head was covered with deer skin and a face was painted on. The hair that had been saved during the year was attached with glue or sewn on with a fine fiber. Images were made to look as much like the deceased individual as possible. Although close relatives made the images, it was the distant people who actually danced with them at the ceremony.

Village men erected a large ramada where the ceremony was to take place. They also dug a very large pit nearby where everything would be burned after the ceremony. Villagers prepared food to take care of literally hundreds of visitors who started arriving the day before the ceremony. This practice was by no means a display of wealth. The concept was much the same as today's funeral. They simply took care of the "out-of-town guests" who had come to pay their last respects.

Ceremonial day found women gathered under the ramada quietly putting finishing touches on the images. In the early evening the men started a huge fire in the pit. People began to gather around. The children ordinarily were not permitted to attend, but Tom was allowed to witness the *last Karuk* because he was the last *Kwaaymii* child. The elders wanted him to remember as many aspects of their culture as possible. Although Tom vividly remembers the ceremony, he was too young to completely understand its profound meaning. The burning of the images at the end of the ceremony scared him and he ran away. His mother sent two fast running Yuma men after him to bring him back.

As night fell, the ritual was ready to begin. The chief and shaman appeared and signaled the start of the ceremony with greetings, prayers and chants. They also started the dancing with other "lead" dancers, either male or female. Tom's grandmother was a lead dancer and was asked to participate because there was no one left at the *Wiiapaayp* village who was qualified to dance the woman's lead dance. The chief and shaman wore special headdresses decorated with eagle and pheasant feathers. The shaman set the pace with his deer hoof rattle and rhythmical singing of the *meskwaa* (special songs or chants). Then the people began to join in the chanting—calling on the spirits, telling them it was time to go on, calling the spirit guides.

Dancers moved counterclockwise around the fire, facing in the direction of their movement. One by one, other dancers with their images joined the circle. Some carried rattles made of hide or gourds and shook them in time with the dance rhythm. No drums were used. When the chief or shaman rested, other lead dancers took over for them.

The singing and dancing continued through the night. Just before dawn, when Venus reached a particular position in the sky, the chief and shaman ended the ceremony. Everyone threw the images and possessions into the big fire pit. The ramada was tom down and burned also. All watched as the flames of the fire billowed upwards toward the sky. Without fail, the smoke always drifted to the south. The spirits had been freed.

There was a solemn hush over the whole area as daylight progressed. Visitors prepared to return to their own villages. From now on the dead would never be talked about—their names never mentioned. Their bodies, spirits and possessions were gone. The *Karuk* was over.

It must be noted here that there was a curious deviation from the *Karuk* at the death of a prominent chief. Particular care was taken to assure that all personal items, especially those that were peculiar to his trade, were burned and buried with his remains. A special *Karuk* ceremony was held one year after his death regardless of the time of year. At the ceremony, a young eagle that had been captured from the nest the previous year was sacrificed for the chief instead of the common image. All attended this religious ceremony which was officiated by the head shaman. The feathers of the sacrificial eagle were passed on to the chief's successor in hopes he too would attain the attributes of the former leader.

Chapter VI

LEGENDS

THE FOLLOWING LEGENDS were told to Mary E. Johnson by Tom's mother, Maria Alto, about 1914. Miss Johnson wrote about Maria, "...whose friendship has been a revelation of the poetic instinct, the dramatic impulse and nobility of character hidden beneath the stoical mask of our primitive people...So swiftly has the hand of civilization wiped out the old traditions and customs, that but few Indians remain who remember them, and fewer still are those willing to divulge them. Only when one comes into intimate contact with them is one accorded the privilege and honor of hearing the tales of their ancestors."

The legends are reprinted here from Mary E. Johnson's booklet, "Indian legends of the Cuyamaca Mountains."

Hilsh Ki'e [*Hillkii*]—The Battle of the Peaks

The Indians claim that Corta Madera Mountain, or Hilsh Ki'e (Pine Tree), as they call it, was once a part of the Cuyamacas, and dwelt in what is now the lower end of Green Valley. They tell a story of a great upheaval of nature which took place in prehistoric times, after which Hilsh Ki'e was discovered far removed from his brother peaks.

***

Many, many ages ago, far beyond recalling, the mighty peaks of Ah-ha' Kwe-ah-mac' [*Ahaa Kwiiamaak*] (Water Beyond) numbered more than now. In those days another peak occupied all the lower part of what is now a fertile valley. Together they raised their shaggy heads in proud triumph o'er the mountains round about them. For the Ah-ha' Kwe-ah-mac' wore beautiful long hair of sweet-smelling pine and cedar trees, and they gazed with disdain upon the others whose heads were covered with short hair of lilac, elm, and such scrub-brush.

A sign of servitude then was short hair. And the long-haired mountains clung close together, never mingling with their inferiors.

There came a time when they quarreled among themselves. No one knew just how it began. Some said it was because the lovely spring Ah-ha' Wi-Ah-ha' [*Ahaawiiahaa*] (Water, Colder Water) betrothed herself to Ahha' Coo-mulk' [*Ahaakomillk*] (Water Sweet), who wished to carry her far below among the short-haired mountains.

The trouble grew. At length they came to blows, and for many days the conflict raged. The great rugged peak Hilsh Ki'e, down through whose arms glided the sparkling river Ah-ha' Coo-mulk', persisted in shielding it. He said that since the little stream was born, he had guarded and cherished it, and he refused to part with it.

Infuriated beyond measure, the other peaks besieged him. They belched out huge rocks upon his head. They leashed his up-turned face with whips of fire from out the sky. And unseen hands snatched up his long strands of hair by the roots.

Sturdily he returned blow for blow, but made no impression on the north peak, nor the middle one, who proved to be exceedingly strong and tough. He managed, however, to twist the head of the south peak and leave a crook in his neck forever. Valiantly he strove against them, but it was an unequal struggle. Finally, in desperation, he gave a mighty wench, freed himself from their fierce embrace and fled.

Out in the deepest darkness of the night he plunged. The crashing thunder and the shrieking wind covered his flight. On and on he sped, never stopping, never heeding that many of his long locks of hair were falling by the way. Through the whole night and all the following day he ran and ran, away from his home.

Exhausted at last, he fell in the midst of the low-browed mountains with short-cropped hair. And that is where you will find him today—grand old Hilsh Ki'e with pine-topped crest and a ragged, jagged, roughhewn scar where he broke off sharp from Ah-ha' Kweah-mac'—there among aliens far, far from his people.

Huts-tah' Tah-mil'tah [*Helltaa Tamilltaa*]—Hanging Head

On the west side of the south peak of the Cuyamacas, far up the old High Trail, is a place called by the Indians, Hutstah' Tah-mil'tah (Hanging Head). The following legend, which has been handed down from time immemorial, explains the naming of the place.

It was the moon of the lilac blossoms in the days long since flown, and all the earth was rousing from the drowsy sleep in which it had lain during the time of the chilling blast. No more did the biting lash of En-yah' Kwik [*inyakwik*] (east wind) sting the cheeks or numb the fingers of the hunter who braved the mountains in search of game. Now, the soft, warm Ka-wak' Kwik [*kawakwik*] (south wind) was blowing, bringing lifegiving showers that filled every little canyon with talking water. Birds were singing their love songs; plants bursting their flower buds; and all nature was teeming with the vigor of Che-pum' [*chiipam*] (spring).

The Indians had returned from their winter sojourn in the balmy air of the coast, and were busily engaged in establishing themselves once again in their village Helshow Na-wa' [*Awaa Kwinyaw*] (Rabbit House) at the base of the towering peak Poo-kwoo-sqwee' [*Puukwuuskwii*] (Crooked Neck);

when a Yuma brave, having found his way across the sands of the desert, came to visit them.

Tall and slender was this brave from a strange tribe, and as straight as an alder. His sinewy body glistened like a red rattler, and his long mane floated out from his head as does gay-colored feathers, red, yellow, and green, and quite rare also were the wings which completed his head dress. Over his shoulders hung a quiver made of wildcat skin, and it was filled with arrows whose heads were carved from the hyacinth and other precious stones found on the edge of the desert.

So superior was his magnificence that, notwithstanding he came with friendly intent, he was the cause of much envy.

One clear day a party of the young warriors escorted him to the top of the high peak to show him the place from whence looking toward En-yak' [*in yak*] (east) he could gaze upon his own, Big Water of the desert, or turning to Ah-wik' [*awik*] (west) behold the Great Sea Water merged in the western skyline.

Glad to find something in which they excelled, they boasted of the greatness of their body of water, decrying the inferiority of his smaller one.

A quarrel ensued in which the Yuma brave was killed. Far up on the mountainside they left his scalp lock with its long streaming hair and gorgeous feathers hanging on the brush. There it fluttered for many a day, the iridescent colors gleaming afar in the sunlight. And, as time passed on, the great spirit of In'ya *[Enyaa]* (Sun) in compassion, transformed it into bright-colored flowers and trailing vines growing among the rocks and brushes.

Now, in that self-same spot, after the blue clouds of lilac bloom have vanished from the hills below, one may see patches of color like a field of tiger-lilies and other brilliant-hued flowers nodding and swaying in the breeze.

Were one strong-armed as the Indians of yore, one could throw a stone from the High Trail straight into that place, and hear mysterious sounds, as did they, when it fell midst the vines and flowers. Sounds, soft and low, as of weird wailing o'er the body of the slain, for the flowers are plaintively chanting the requiem of Huts-tah' Tah-mil'tah.

Ah-ha' Wi-Ah-ha' [*Ahaawiiahaa*]—Water Colder Water

The Cold Spring, located on the high peak of the Cuya-macas, is well known to all lovers of these mountains, and the Indians, who must ever have a reason for the existence of things, tell how it was created and named by one of their mythical creatures of long ago.

A t one time in the ages past, the Ah-ha' Kwe-ah-mac' mountains were infested by monstrous giants with loathsome, ill-shaped bodies, who terrorized the surrounding country. These marauders, lurking and watching their opportunity, frequently stole the Indian maids from their villages, keeping them in bondage as slaves.

One of the giants, named Hum-am' Kwish'wash [*Hamam Kwishwash*] (Whip to Kill People), lived in the vicinity of Green Valley.

He reveled in the most fiendish ogrisms [sic], but his innate sense of the beautiful was keen and strong. He not only selected the most delightful places in which to live, but surrounded himself with objects pleasing to the eye. Always he stole the fairest of the Indian maids, and required them to weave the most exquisite designs known in their art of basket making.

His cruelty was extreme, and did his slaves displease him in the least, they met with the most horrible death imaginable.

This hideous being possessed supernatural powers which he employed in various ways. It seems he that [sic] wanted nothing but the coldest water to drink. He tried the water in the streams, and tried the water in the springs which abound throughout the country, but never did any of it suit his taste; so he created for himself a spring of colder water.

In one of the most alluring spots on the mountain side, in the dense shade of the fragrant forest of pines and cedars, he brought forth a crystal spring of icy water, and named it Ah-ha' Wi-Ah-ha'.

Here in this nook of surpassing loveliness, where the graceful lilies nod their stately heads, and delicate fronds of lacelike greenery push their way up through the carpet of velvet moss, he sent his slaves with their beautifully woven water baskets to fetch him a drink when he grew thirsty.

One day, calling a slave he commanded her to bring some water instantly, with dire threats of punishment should it become insipid before it reached him.

This maiden, radiant with the beauty of the starlight, was so good, so pure, so true, that she had been fairly adored by her people before she was so cruelly snatched from their midst.

Swiftly she wound her way up through the towering aisles of solemn pines, softly intoning their prayers to the heavens above them. Wistfully longing to be free from the dreadful ogre who held her captive, she begged the trees to plead with the great In'ya, who rules over all, to take pity on her distress.

The flowers and the birds felt the quivering throb of her anguish. The starry-eyed snowflowers, gleaming in the shade by the wayside, gave their incense to be wafted on high by the whispering breeze; the cooing dove sent its most plaintive cry above; and every other living thing along the pathway offered its gift in her behalf to In'ya riding the heavens in his flaming ball of light.

When she reached the spring she sat on its brink, and filled her basket with its cold, refreshing water. Gazing into the crystal depths she caught a glimmer of a shadow quickly passing, and at once knew it to be that of the good spirit of the spring.

She beseeched and plead with it to save her from the clutches of Hum-am' Kwish'wash; and, as she leaned over farther and farther, trying to get one more glimpse of the shadow, the waters rose up and gently engulfed her.

All nature hushed in a sweet silence of gratitude as she was drawn into the protecting arms of Ah-ha' Wi-Ahha'; and there she has dwelt in safety ever since.

Ah Kwer-rup' [*Aakwerap*]—Disease Cure

Near the place called Huts-tah' Tah-mil'tah, on the west side of Cuyamaca Peak in an almost inaccessible spot, is a huge, white rock, as large as a house. It looks as if it might have been sprinkled with blood, for it is flecked with spots of bright red, and a sharp cleft divides it in twain.

The name of this rock is Ah Kwer-rup' (disease cure). In ancient times the Indians believed that it possessed the power to dispel aches and pain, and the medicine men took their sick, who were suffering from any painful malady, there to be healed.

Wonderful and miraculous were some of the cures said to have been performed there. But in time it lost its power and fell into disuse.

However, some of the Indians say, that even now, if one gets near enough to fling a stone against the big rock, it sings or cheeps like a young birdling; and they still hold it in reverence.

Hul-ya-oo' Nimoo-lu'kah [*Huulyaw Nimuuluukaa*]—Phantom Basket

On this same enchanted side of the mountain is another great rock, which no one has ever succeeded in reaching on account of the dense brush and sharp rocks surrounding it.

On top of this rock, just at the break of day, suddenly is seen an immense basket filled with eagle feathers and wings of the black crow sticking up in the center. Its appearance varies. Sometimes the basket is very beautiful and new, and the feathers shining and bright as though freshly plucked from the birds; again it looks old and dingy, and the feathers are dull and frayed at the tip.

No one has ever been able to reach the place, but many are the Indians who have gone up the High Trail before sunrise to behold the phantom basket appear on top of the rock.

Na-wa Ti'e [*Awaataay*]—Big House

Mount Guatay or Na-wa Ti'e as the Indians call it, lies near Descanso, only a few miles distant from Cuyamaca Peak. It looms up from all points of view like a giant wigwam built for some great chieftain of the Golden Age. Its massive frame is royally covered by a thick robe of velvet verdure, with plumes of rarest cypress along the northern ridges.

The glory and peace and silence of its broad expanse is ever the same, whether raised to the smiling sun or draped in the filmy gauze of evening's amethyst veil.

Seemingly it might be inhabited by a benign spirit of guardianship, as it looks so serenely and calmly o'er the valley bearing its name. But in the days when the village Hum-poo' Ar-rup'ma (Whip of the Wind) in the upper edge of the valley rang with sounds of busy activity, it was entirely different.

Then the comely Indian maids, pounding their acorn meal in the mortars on the rocky knoll of the village, were fearful of incurring the displeasure of Na-wa Ti'e. Even the valiant warriors, brave in their fierce array, dared not ascend the mountain side or pluck one branch of the rare trees growing there.

For to Na-wa Ti'e, was given the power of creating the penetrating wind, the blighting frost, the freezing snow, and the driving sleet. When enraged it caused the spirit of Ha-choor' [*Hiichur*] (Cold) to spring from out the center of its heart chilling the marrow of their bones, and carrying devastation throughout the fertile valley.

So one and all gazed on it with awe; molesting it not, never venturing up its slopes; ever fearful, ever dreading, lest they might arouse the ire of Na-wa Ti'e.

94

In-yar'en Ah-ha'—No Eyes in Water

A spring which rises in the edge of the river flat at Descanso is pointed out by the Indians as one in which dwells a bad spirit. The following tale concerns its evil power.

A ll night long those who were awake heard the uncanny screams of Kwin Mari' (Blind Baby), who dwelt in the bewitched spring of In-yar'en Ah-ha', which oozed from the muddy bank and trickled down a sedgy flat to the river. Sharp, distressing sounds they were, like the cries of a frightened baby, and left a shuddering fear in the hearts of all who listened in the little village of Pilch'com-wa (White as Ashes).

This village, so called because nearly every morning the frost caused the ground to appear as though powdered with ashes, was just west of the river, and so near the evil spring that the piercing wails penetrated the remotest wigwam.

Old squaws of fearless mein listened with bated breath; young mothers clasped their little ones closer in shivering fear, thinking how they might perchance have been born under the blight of Kwin Mari'; and those dear women who were living in daily hope of giving a beautiful, brave man-child to their people, cowered in agony on their pallets of fur, drawing the soft robes closer about their heads to deaden the shrill cries.

All who heard knew that the spirit of Kwin Mari' was seeking a victim. Even the children knew that it could cast a spell over the mother before her little one entered the world, which would seal its eyes to earthly sight forever. So throughout the night they lay in waking dread.

As the first grey line of dawn pushed up through the blackness of the night the cries ceased, and a strange woman crept into the village faintly calling for help.

Eagerly the people succored her; and, when her strength returned, she told how those in her own village had been killed by foes, she alone escaping.

How, after wandering about for several days, she had heard in the night just passed, the screams of a baby in distress, and set out at once to find it. Stumbling in the dark, over rocks and thorny brush, she at last entered an open space soft under foot with the touch of new grown grass. As she drew nearer and nearer to the sounds, she reached a bank, mucky and wet. Here she stooped down to pick up the baby, thinking she had found it; but her hands plunged into a pool of water instead, and, as the sharp cries rose again from her very feet, she fell back paralyzed with fear.

Not until dawn had she been able to move. Then she crawled to the nearest wigwam which she saw rising ghost-like on the hill before her. Little did she know what had befallen her; but the people, who well knew, kept her with them caring for her tenderly till her little one was born.

Only after she had seen how tightly closed were his tiny eye-lids, resisting all efforts to open them, did they tell her of Kwin Mari', dwelling in the bewitched spring of In-yar'en Ah-ha', and how it had the power, could it but touch the mother, of blinding her little unborn babe.

Seen-u-how' How-wak' [*Siinyahaw Haawak*]—Old Woman's Twins

A mysterious woman figures largely in the myths connected with the Laguna mountains, which lie adjacent to the Cuyamacas on the east. These are probably of as ancient origin as any now in the remembrance of the Indians, and date far back to the time when the animals were the brothers of man, speaking his language, and the various deities were of miraculous birth.

From out of En-Yak' [*inyak*] (east) no one knows how, nor when, nor where, came a woman, and dwelt in a cave in the mountains, and her name was Seen-uhow'. This happened in the long forgotten days, and no one can tell exactly how she looked. Sometimes she was young and beautiful; again she appeared as a wizened, old hag, feeble, and bent with age. One only knows that she existed from the beginning of time, possessing the power of dispelling her age by bathing in Ah-ha' Kwe'se-i [*ahaa kwisiiyaay*] (bewitched water).

She lived alone in her cave, and one morning when she went down to an enchanted pool of clear spring water to bathe and renew her youth, she found Howwak' floating on the bosom of its limpid pureness. In those days man was not born of woman, but sprang in infancy from the living water of crystal springs.

Home to her cave she took the twin boys and that night they grew in some marvelous, mysterious manner to full-fledged manhood; but as different as are the deepest twilight shadows from the rose-light blush of dawn.

The one she named Par-a-han' [*Parahaan*] was pensive and sad of heart, while the other, called Sat-e-co' [*Saatiiko*], sparkled with laughter and song.

Many, many ages did they live in the cave with Seenu-how', never growing any older, neither did their dispositions vary. Par-a-han' was always sorrowful, Sat-e-co' ever gay.

From the young shoots of an elderberry bush they fashioned a flute on which Sat-e-co' played joyous melodies as he wandered far and near o'er the country. Haunting, rippling, lilting, little tunes that floated off on the breeze.

One day two Indian maids, in the far distance, heard the echo of those seductive tones and stole away from their people to follow the enchanting strains. Finally reaching the place where dwelt Seen-u-how' with her sons, they became enamored of the How-wak'; and they staid and became their wives.

Yet they dared not remain away from their people for any length of time, for fear they might be followed and punished. For the Chief, their father, had heard of the woman of magic and her queer sons, and forbidden any of his tribe to go near them.

So, regretfully telling Par-a-han' and Sat-e-co' goodbye, and promising to come back to them as quickly as possible, the two Indian women returned to their home, never saying where they had been.

Their father, who was an exceedingly wise man, surmised the truth, however, and kept close guard over them lest they go again. He knew that after awhile the How-wak' would come seeking, and then he could kill them.

Darkness followed the light, and time went on. Par-ahan' and Sat-e-co' grew tired of waiting and told Seen-u-how' that they intended to search for their women and bring them back to live in the cave again.

Seen-u-how', knowing all things ere they happened, warned them of the Chieftain's anger; begged them not to go, and foretold the horrible manner in which death would overtake them.

Heeding not her warning, and feeling sure of outwitting the Chief, nothing could dissuade them. But before setting out on their journey across the wilderness of mountains, they twisted a long rope from the strong fibre of the mescal plant, stretching it taut from one pine tree to another in front of their cave. They told their mother, should any evil befall them, the rope would break in the center and one end fly to Ka-tulch' [*kaatuch*] (north) and the other fly to Ka-wak' [*kaawak*] (south). Then they started off to find their wives.

The trail was long and beset with many difficulties. When they reached the border of the great Chief's domain, they laid [sic] down to rest before making the final dash after his daughters. But he, with some of his warriors, discovered them while they slept, and seized them, putting them to death after the most hideous tortures.

Seen-u-how', desolate and forsaken in the cave, knew they were dead ere she peered out of the gloom and beheld the rope of mescal parted in twain, the one end having flown to the north, and the other to the south.

Loudly, and long she wailed and wept for her departed How-wak'. Then in anguish disappeared in En-yak' mysteriously as she had arrived—no one knows how, nor when, nor where.

But there is a point on Ah-ha' Mut-ta-ti'e [*Ahaa Mutataay*] (Water Mountains) where one may stand and look out across the vast stretches of desert sand while the mystic shades of night are deepening, and see a light in the far east, a light like the flicker of a torch. As one looks it illumines a cave in which sits an old woman, haggard and shriveled, and all alone, then her image vanishes. Looking again one sees the form of a beautiful maiden, in all the glory of her youth; her long, black hair shines in the glimmering light, and the beads of her necklace sparkle like twinkling stars. She too, is alone, and fades away.

It is Seen-u-how' dwelling in En-yak', and there she renews her youth from time to time by bathing in the dew of the fleecy clouds which float about her.

Seen-u-how' Hum-poo' [*Siinyahaw Hampuu*]—Old Woman's Whip

Another story of the Lagunas tells how Seen-u-how' marked the birds and animals with her Hum-poo' (whip). The Hum-poo' is a stick of tough wood shaped like a half circle and very sharp at one end. The Indians could throw the Hum-poo' with great accuracy and often used it to kill game.

Somewhere on the precipitous side of Ah-ha' Mut-tati'e where the atmosphere quivers with a mystical radiance, and rocks assume fantastic shapes, is a cave formed like a half moon. Seen-u-how', the old woman of magic, lived there in olden times with her How-wak'; one of whom was so happy and light-hearted that he laughed and sang the whole day long, while the other was exceedingly quiet and sad, spending most of his time in the dark shadows of the cave bemoaning his fate.

The joyous son wandered back and forth o'er the mountains day after day. Free from care he roamed, making friends with the birds and animals, talking with them, and learning their wisdom. They, in turn, became devoted to him, often following him home, even staying there at times when he was on distant journeys.

In those days the animals resembled each other so closely (as did the birds also), that they could hardly be told apart, and they all had the gift of speech.

But Seen-u-how' and the sorrowful son never said a word to them, though at times so many congregated there that the cave was crowded to overflowing.

The animals could see, however, the weird, mysterious things which transpired there in the dim light. Sometimes they looked at the wrinkled face of old Seen-u-how' and she changed into a beautiful maiden, clad in finest buckskin, wearing strings of glittering beads around her neck, on her feet were moccasins woven from the mescal plant, such as the fleet runners wore on long journeys, and she seemed short of breath as though having come swiftly a long distance. Meanwhile, the son of the saddened heart softly wailed and mourned out his dismal life.

One day, when most of the people of the animal world had gathered in the cave, Huta-pah' [*Haatipaa*] (Coyote) felt a drop of water splash on his face. He whispered to the other people that it must be raining. The shadows were so deep he could not see that the woe-be-gone son sat weeping near him in the gloom.

The others thought Huta-pah' was mistaken, but said he, "Hush! listen! and you can hear the drops falling." And listening, they did hear the patter of the tear-drops falling from the eyes of the sorrowful one, yet knew not what it was. So they all rushed through the low opening of the cave to see if it really was raining.

This angered Seen-u-how' and, as they dashed by her, she struck each one with her Hum-poo'; not killing any, but greatly changing their appearance, however.

She made three marks down the back of Ma-pa'cha [*Mahwaa*] (Badger); tore the tail of Huta-pah' (Coyote) and now it is bushy instead of long and pointed; pounded Nim-me' [*Naamii*] (Wildcat) so hard that the marks of the blows remain on its body yet; Quck [*Akwak*] (Deer) carried a long tail before it was whacked off by the Hum-poo'; poor To-Iuk' [*Aaya'uu*] (Owl) had his eyes so injured that he only sees by night since then; even the smallest bird of all, with its ruby colored throat, shows where it felt the flick of the whip.

Scarcely a beast or a bird of the wildwood but received that day some mark of Seen-u-how's Humpoo', and that is the reason they can be distinguished one from another.

Kwut'ah Lu'e-ah-Song Dance

One of the ancient rites performed in by-gone days by the Indians dwelling in the village Helsh-ow' Na-wa' (Rabbit House) at the foot of the Cuyamaca Peak was the Kwut'ah Lu'e-ah given in honor of In'ya (Sun). The summit of Viejas mountain, just on the other side of their village, was chosen as the place for this celebration to be held,* and they named the mountain Kwut'ah Lu'e-ah on account of it.

Long before Kwut'ah Lu'e-ah mountain fell into the hands of See-i (Evil One), the Indians made a pilgrimage once a year to its very top to watch In'ya come out of En-yak', and praise and honor him with song and dance. For In'ya was the great Ruler of All Things. He governed the universe; he commanded the earth; nothing grew unless he caused it; he even dominated the bodies of men, some of whom he made energetic and strong, others weak and lazy. When he disappeared at night he cast a drowsiness o'er the world, so that everything slept until it was time for him to come again in the morning. Such a great ruler as he, 'received due reverence and worship.

For many preceding moons the young Braves prepared themselves for the race which began the celebration of Kwut'ah Lu'e-ah. They ate no meat, nuts, or oily substance while in' training for this event, and daily they bathed and rubbed their bodies with Cha-hoor' (Clear Rock). This crystal of the nature of alum, made them light on their feet like animals, so they could jump over high boulders and run with the swiftness of deer.

*Note: Some time ago a team of archaeologists confirmed the presence of a prehistoric observatory located on top of Viejas Mountain. From the position of key rocks located within the stone circle, they had determined then that the feature had been previously used to observe the summer solstice, the longest day of the year. A year later the same team returned to the site for further study and found the site had been completely destroyed by campers. All the rocks within the circle had been removed and fashioned into modern camping hearths where once the observatory had been situated.

When the time came, everything was in readiness. The big circle on top of the mountain had been freshly prepared and cleared for the dancers and singers. The aged and feeble, with the small children of the village, had been carefully carried up there the previous afternoon, that they might be on hand to take part in the ceremonies.

Then, in that mystic hour which is neither night, nor day, the able-bodied ones made the ascent. Last of all, after the others had reached the top, the runners came; swiftly they vied with each other over the steep trails—some so fleet they seemed to fly like birds over the course.

When all had reached the summit, the ritualistic ceremonies began. With song and dance in the blushing dawn, they watched for In'ya, Ruler of All. Opalescent streamers of golden radiance and flaming banners of crimson flaunting across the pearly tints of the receding night, heralded his arrival; while the people chanted songs of praise in honor of his wonderful light, and made obeisance in the dance in homage of his great power over all things.

Year after year this celebration took place till See-i grew envious, and cast a spell over the mountain; then the Indians feared to make the ascent any more.

One or two foolhardy ones made the attempt, but they found the trails tedious and wearisome. The springs of water by the pathway were poisonous, and frightful noises like the hissing and rattle of snakes pursued their footsteps, and they gave up in despair.

So, though the old trails are faintly discernible and traces of the ring where they danced and sung still remain, no more does the red man swiftly ascend Kwut'ah Lu'e-ah mountain to watch In'ya come out of En-yak' in all his glory.

Ah Kwir [*Aakwer*]—Red Paint

Ah Kwir is the name of a war paint which was made from very fine dirt taken from a hill somewhere out on the desert.* It was of great value when the warriors painted their faces and bodies with the insignia of their tribe. The desert Indians were accustomed to bring it with other desert products up to the mountains to barter in trade with the tribes living there.

One of the numerous "Coyote stories" of the Indians living on the Cuyamacas gives their version of how this famous Ah Kwir came into existence.

Huta-pah' (Coyote) the meanest man who ever lived, was waiting and watching for his feeble, old father to die. He told the people that he wanted to watch until death came so he might see that the body of his beloved father was properly burned and given ceremonial burial. But the people knew what a liar he was, and that he only wanted to be there that he might devour the body of his father.

So Orse [Oso or *Naamuul*] (Bear) said, "No! Nim-me' and Quck and the rest of the people will watch by the side of your sick father. You go off and hunt for something to eat, you are always hungry."

He sulked and whined, but they made him go, and slowly he loped down the trail. Shortly he returned, saying he could not find a thing to eat. Surmising he that [sic] had only been hiding in the bushes waiting his father's death, they sent him away once more. Again he came back with nothing, and repeated this performance till they lost all patience, and finally

---

*Note: In 1980, a large deposit of iron oxide was found during a survey of the western Imperial Valley desert. It is located at the eastern foot of the Coyote Mountains near the Mexican border. This deposit is only a stone's throw off the major east-west corridor which linked the mountain Indians to their desert counterparts. Maria Alto had told Tom of an area in the desert where "*aakwer*" came from, but Tom had never been there. To date, this is the only deposit of iron oxide known in the area, and because of prehistoric artifacts found in association with the site, as well as its location along the main mountain-desert trail, it would seem probable that the deposit was used by prehistoric peoples.

they said, "Go far, far away and hunt. If you dare return before In'ya takes his night rest, we shall kill you."

This time he really went a long distance, for, with all his sly, crafty ways, he was a big coward and their threats frightened him.

His father died while he was gone, and the people started a fire as quickly as possible, and began burning the body in order that it might be consumed before Huta-pah' got back.

Now he was many miles away when the smoke from that funeral pyre rose up through the tall pines, and drifted off on the breeze, but his keen nose scented it, and he turned back at a great rate of speed.

Orse and Quck and Nim-me' and the other people heard him coming, and drew close together in a circle round the fire, guarding the dead body of his father.

Shrieking and wailing as he drew near, he cried, "I must see my dear father once more before all is burned up." But they paid no heed to his cries for they knew what a bad man he was.

Then, in his crafty way, he discovered that there was a low place in the defensive circle where Nim-me' stood, for he, you know, is quite a short person; so Huta-pah' sneaked back in the brush, made a running jump over Nim-me's head and landed by the side of his father's body.

Snatching out the heart from the glowing embers of fire, away he dashed. Across valleys and mountains he ran, and far out on the desert sands.

Finally, he stopped on a hill on the other side, and ate up the heart of his father. As the red drops of blood slowly oozed from his cruel jaws and fell to the ground beneath, the entire hillside assumed a ruddy hue. And to this day, the earth there retains the color of the blood which dripped from the heart of Huta-pah's father.

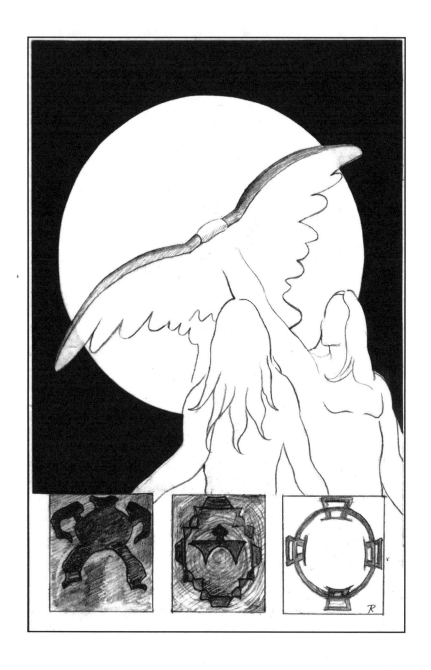

Chapter VII

THE SPIRIT WORLD

Creation

TOM LUCAS HAS PROVIDED information on legends and my-
thology in addition to that which we have reprinted from his
mother's stories as told to Mary E. Johnson. I chose to quote
Mr. Lucas directly in his explanation of *Kwaaymii* myths and
their understanding of the spirit world.

"The great one above put life into our dirt bodies, which
means that some time way back the body was made from the
dirt and the Great Spirit put the life into it—out of this soil,
right here. We call the Great Spirit *Amaayahaa*. We have all
the belief in the world that creation made our people right
here, not in Europe or anywhere else—right here, where they
belong, not anywhere else. If they made them over in another
country, there was no incentive for them to come and sail a
great ocean and get over here, but that's still a controversial
thing. After man and woman was made, the life was blown
into them. It was the breath that was given. Well, the breath
could be anything. It could be just a command to be a person.

"Of course, science says the Indian comes from somewhere else, from over the Bering Straits. But that don't jive
with the Indians themselves. There isn't a one yet that I ever

knew that claimed any part whatsoever with coming [here]. They feel that the creation put them here, that this was the place and there was different things. The legend is that there has been times when there was a great teacher on the earth, and he lived [gave life to] things. They were all created in this country and they were given the different signs to go by, the different stars and their positions in the mornings and evenings, and that's how they know just when to plant, and the Indians living in the desert in the winter know just when to start moving back to their other countries, the higher mountains—their home.

"I was pretty young when I heard all those stories, but there was a great being that put them here and they always believed in that. But just like anything else, there was the adverse beings too that always came on in to divert their minds to baser things. The true Indian, the follower of *Amaayahaa*, for instance, had a respectable name for every part of the body, while the other kind of people had some foul names for every darn thing else. There was a definite dividing line between the two.

"There were the Indians that were destructive and have gone out to raid and have kidnapped younger people to trade off or something. Some of these California Indians have had the experience. They must have been taken far north and traded two or three times to different tribes. Sometimes the people could get away and find their way back to their own people.

"Anyway, the Indians believed in the spiritual. When your body got old it would go back to the earth from whence it's made—from the dirt, from the ashes. The story is almost the same as your Bible.

"So, the Indian was created right here...Why did the Creator have to go and create people over in the cradle of civilization around Europe and Asia and never create nothing over in this country? It don't quite make any sense. They're entirely different people. Take like in Africa, those dark races and all—they were supposed to be marked this color for some reason. We were marked too, for some reason. Maybe it's a mark of distinction or maybe it's just because we live in this country.

"Our bodies are from the earth and the light is blown into us and we go forth and propagate and teach. Everything was supposed to have gone good until some of the adverse things. According to the legend, this man of the adverse standing, he was quite a wizard at everything. He also knows how to foretell everything, but he was strictly a cannibalistic type. They claim that there was a time way in the early days, that far up north along the coast, there were some kind of man-eating people that were detested and abhorred, and thought they might some day come down this far. Apparently they never did. Now, that might have been something that migrated over here. I don't know."

Animals and Birds

"The deer and rabbit and game, well, that was a provision made for humans to exist but without overdoing, without slaughtering them all. All the animals had a reason to be what they are. The humans all came from the original one and they multiplied and they didn't do right and they were changed into animals.

"For instance, there's a blackbird with the red wing and that was supposed to be a human that went around with his shoulder painted …and that blackbird carried his mark to this day. There's the road runner who, as a human, got hit over the head and he had a bloody stripe on his head and he carries that mark to this day, too.

"The pheasant was always a bird and he kept his beautiful feathers. The legend is that the creator made this beautiful bird to fly in the heavens. The eagle was the chief. He is considered the closest, spiritually, to a human. He is chief of all the birds now. They aren't exactly worshipped, but there's a lot of respect for that bird. They would climb up to a nest and get the young eagles. They kept them in a cage and fed them and cared for them so they could have the feathers. If ever the eagle died or was sacrificed, they say that there was just about as big a mourning as if a person died. He commanded respect among the Indians, and he still does to this day. The eagle was cremated in the early days but later on he was buried just like the humans.

"Eagles always go back to the same nest, the same area. The chiefs and shamans go where the eagles are for the meditations. They say there's supposed to be some special markings up there on that Table Mountain [eastern San Diego County]. Word always gets around about those special places—always. It's really pretty old [the Table Mountain area], maybe one thousand years or so. It looks like a place for rituals, an ideal place. I went up there just recently—don't know for sure where those markings are but I sure saw the eagle's nest. There was a new nest built on top of an old one, and there was an even older nest right next to it. As we watched, the mother eagle took off to draw our attention away from the nest. Then, one by one, there were four young eagles that took off after the mother. Oh, it was the most wonderful thing to watch. They circled around over head for a few minutes, then gradually disappeared. You could tell which one was the mature bird by her longer wing feathers. We took pictures of them.

"Sometimes if a big chief or somebody worthwhile passes away, then they keep an eagle for a year, take his feathers, and in commemoration of that man's death at the end of the year, they sacrifice the eagle. That was a big mourning. The chief of all the birds was a chief of all the people at one time and turned into a bird. No commoner was rightfully represented by an eagle."

The Human Spirit

"They thought that the opening [the fontanel] left a better contact with the spirit that was delivered to them. The spirit is the invisible person that stays with that child, that person, all his life until he passes away; then the spirit leaves.

"After the baby's head closes up the spirit still remains at the head. It's just like an invisible thread that goes and comes into your head. The life itself, according to the Indian story, is supposed to enter through the head because that's the most sensitive, the most supreme gift there is—your brains. Without your brains you can't think of nothing—your heart won't think, your belly won't think. So, the spirit goes out of the body at the head, too."

Animism

"Things had some certain life. Like they say, you go out and you have to talk to the plant. For instance, you had a very bad bruised leg or something and you were out in the woods. You go out and get the best poultice I know—jimson weed. I'd ask the Great Spirit that gave us that plant [to give us] the plant. Then I tell the spirit of the plant that I was going to use part of that plant to do an awful lot of good and I'd like its help. They didn't do that so much with gathering acorns, because they had already fallen from the tree. But they did give thanks to the Great Spirit for the good crop they have in the morning that they leave to gather. To the east, the west, the north, the south—they're thankful for it.

"They had regular names for the spirits [of the four directions]. The wind from the east brings us warmth and sunlight; out to the west it goes, which brings on the night for the rest of all. The north wind brings us the rain and the storms, the water that we need. The south gives us comfort, warmth. Surprisingly, the tribe that believes that and goes along with it got along pretty good even with the trying times with what little they had. The Shoshone ritual was very similar.

"Until the advent of other religion that was introduced to them, so many of the Indians became very much confused and after awhile they don't believe in either one.

"The rock shrine on the main trail is representative of the spirit that looks after the journeys. There's more shrines up in the Chocolate Mountains and that's the real testing ground. From there you go out into the Mojave Desert. It's an awful long ways to water.

"During the gathering time, the learned men and women get together and it was just a song and that was bringing

111

down a thank you for the gift from the Great Creator to be enlightened, so that the wind might be to their back, pathways may be clear of pebbles and thorns—thankful for the game, for the deer—may the spirits of all the game be taken on to the happy, happy land of the lush feed, where they never feel no heat, no arrow…I can't remember all of it but it went like that. I often wondered after I got old enough to hunt deer and stuff—by golly, I have to think twice before I go out and kill a deer. I do what I have to, and many times I hunted. I didn't do it for no pleasure and I never enjoyed it.

"Animals have spirits just as well as anybody else, and it's been known more than one time, that there's been different manifestations. After killing a deer, you ask the Great Supreme Being to take care of the spirit of the deer and to take it to a happy place—it has done its duty; it has paid the utmost good it's intended for. It will give us food and health and strength. You don't have to say that out loud, you can think it. But mean it if you say it. Mean every word of it.

"We never kill an animal without telling its spirit that we are thankful that it was put here to feed us and that we wish it to go on to a land that's plentiful where it will never again be disturbed—to its happiest days—and you send them off with a good thought. We always did that to any animal or bird or fish. A lot of people don't think of that. They just run out there and shoot them. We don't have the right to just go out and kill an animal. They have a right to live but they also have a reason to be here—to furnish food. So, we're thankful for that and we're thankful to the Good Spirit that he provided us with those things. Surprising how it works. There ain't nothing foolish about it at all"

Spirits of the Dead

"We are given the life and by living right and doing right we shall be like a seed of the sage. But when we do things that are in the adversity to the Creator, things isn't so good. If you make things die, you shall die. You waste things and you shall be wasted. Actually, it's just about like do unto others what you'd like to be done to you. Take care of your people that have passed on, and help them and they'll help you. If you're in need of something, some information, and it comes to you, well, that's a manifestation of that, and I've seen it. I wouldn't be able to contest that at all.

"I was just a boy, about thirteen, and I used to go and bring the cows in for milking time. Riding down the trail, the cattle and my horse wanted to really go. It was all I could do to hang on. We came past a log where one old man used to go there during the day. He didn't belong there but he came there for his health. I guess he was pretty sick. He was gone about a year down to his home. I looked up there and I could see that old man sitting there. He had a brown hat and he was kind of grinning. I looked at him just once. I saw him. I couldn't stop. My ol' horse just kept taking me right on down there. And as soon as I got home I told them that old man is over here and I wondered when he came—he was there cutting wood. So, mother said she had to go over to ol' Juan's [Juan Baptiste, the medicine man] and find out what's going on like the back country people do. So she went over there and Juan said he didn't know nothing—hadn't seen the old man since he left here a year ago; that he was feeling pretty bad and didn't think he'd be back here again. My mother told Juan that I'd seen him that morning sawing some wood. My mother thought maybe I was telling a story. But you can't fool Old Lady Gertrude [Juan's wife]. She said to wait, not to say anything to me—wait a week or so. I had a feeling too. So they let it go. By golly, the next day comes a messenger that said that old man died and they wanted Juan to come down there and recite the rosary for him. Juan was good at that. That old man always talked to me and was friendly to me and I kind of liked the old fellow. And then he just showed himself to me when he died. But I wasn't scared or nothing. I was happy to see him. I was going back there later to see him.

"Yep, my mother thought I just made up a story to be able to go over there, but Old Lady Gertrude must have had a premonition about him dying because she said to wait and find out. Well, you see those things just being out in nature, just

Maria Alto. c. 1914.

living with nature, and I tell you it's more wonderful than anything else.

"After Juan passed away, I used to hear him and his horse, you know, for about a year after he died. He was an expert rider and used to train horses. He used to have a favorite horse. I'm telling you, when you'd get on that horse, it would make the seat of your Levis smile! There were a lot of spirits in that canyon [the trail connecting the villages]. My wife saw a man there, an old man with ragged clothes. When she looked again, he was gone. Sometimes when the wind blows down that trail, you can hear crying and wailing of an old woman. It sounds like my grandmother."

Spirit Helpers

"Well, the way I understand it, is that life is never dead —never. They're past masters of spirits and all that. Well, they still are, a lot of them, but you don't hear about them—not as much as you do with the white people. The white people learn a few things and they start up a booth and tell fortunes. It has to be more or less born within a person to be able to talk with the spirits. You have to be able to bring it on through, and you have to be able to understand and see what a person is good for."

Omens

"To see an eagle means something good, something better. A hoot owl will bring you a message—if he comes over to your house or sits on your house or if he happened to be on your trail. I know a woman who worked at Santa Ysabel. She got paid one day and was on her way home to the Julian area. On her trail, a hoot owl kept landing in front of her, and about the third time, she was near the open country. She had a funny feeling about it and decided to get off the trail and sit down in the brush, hidden from the trail. Pretty soon, she saw two men running up the trail behind her. They went about half way across the valley and stopped because they figured she couldn't have gone that fast ahead of them. They started to come back and she moved on through the brush as far off the trail as she could get. She said if she hadn't gotten off that trail, they would have overtaken her and stolen her money. There were men watching her when she left the place she worked, at the old Santa Ysabel trading post.

"The rattlesnake delivers a warning beforehand. It usually means death in the family. We had one that came right up around our water olla, just laid itself out in front of our house. That was just before my grandmother died. My mother said it wasn't a rattlesnake, but a spirit taking over the snake to warn us. No snake would have gone there. At that time there wasn't a bush around to attract a rattlesnake. It had been all cleared out."

Dreams

"These are related to premonitions. They ask the guiding spirit [their own] to tell them something in dream that they're supposed to know."

Legend of the *Kwaaymii* Bird

"It means the name of the bird that sings. Well, that bird became extinct. It was supposed to have been something like a hawk and built something like a hawk, only it had beautiful, green, iridescent feathers, something like a parrot's feathers, but it was not a parrot. It was considered a high, sacred bird and one of the greatest creations. Whenever the song is heard, whenever it's seen, it's supposed to bring a premonition that something eventually is going to be happening—usually a warning. It was claimed that that bird lived in the spring because different ones of the tribe saw it. It didn't mean no harm. It didn't sing any song that would cast out any wrong foretelling of anything to come except only at a time during the big meeting—gathering, big feast. That song was heard

116

in the air and from then on there was a big sickness that hit that country and just about wiped out all of it. So, the bird actually was used often times in the song of some old Indian meetings. They mentioned his name, they mentioned that it was one of their favorite birds of the Great Kingdom of the heavens above. Wherever it comes from, wherever it lives, it never dies. All it is is a spirit bird, but you actually never see it and never will touch it. So, apparently what they did see of him, it was not a bird in reality, but it was just a spiritual bird that you see only in a vision. It might have been some of the learned people amongst the Indians. It was just a spirit bird.

"I thought I've seen the bird too, but I don't know if it was the one or not. I saw it when my grandmother passed on. It was kind of a big hawk and he flew right up and he turned and went away. It was kind of a shiny thing—it just disappeared down toward the spring. Of course, this was my grandmother's home, her place for years and years, and naturally it would have come back to tell about her too."

120

Chapter VIII

INFLUENCE OF MISSIONARIES AND SETTLERS

THE LIFE OF THE CALIFORNIA INDIAN was to change drastically after the establishment of the first mission in San Diego in 1769. Although the *Kwaaymii* lived high in the Laguna Mountains, it didn't take long for them to get news of the coast that came by way of runners.

Hundreds of young people were lured into the clutches of the padres on the pretext of teaching them the ways of farming and, under the watchful eye of the Spanish soldiers, they were held against their wills. If they tried to escape, they were caught, brought back and beaten into submission. One way or another, the padres were going to teach the Indians the ways of "civilized" man and his religion.

The Indians revolted that same year. Many fled their homeland seeking refuge with their mountain neighbors. Some continued into the desert areas and others moved as far east as the Colorado River with the Yuma people. A few joined with the Chemehuevi, Cahuilla and Cupeño tribes to the north.

By 1781, the Spanish were making new routes across the mountains, rummaging through Indian camps and villages, looking for gold and silver. Mr. Lucas says, "Before the

Spanish, they [the Indians] used to have gold and silver—not from here but it was traded. They didn't have a lot—maybe an amulet on a necklace. But when the Spanish came, the word got around about that gold and silver and the Indians buried that and forgot about it. They weren't going to give that to nobody. That was used to torture many an Indian to death— just good, honest people—just to find out where some more of that gold is."

Mr. Lucas had an uncle whose great-grandmother remembered when the Spanish took over San Diego area. Mission influence spread steadily and the Indians began to discard their old beliefs and customs. A few hung on trying to preserve what they had, passing it on to new generations, sometimes in secret. "So, that's the reason why the California Indians kind of lost out on their original songs and customs and all, because of the missionaries."

Maria Alto—1910.

In 1860, a smallpox epidemic, brought with the influx of white settlers, decimated the Indian population. According to Kroeber (1974), the population of Diegueño and Kamia groups between 1770 and 1910 had fallen about 75%. Cattlemen were looking for grazing lands for their herds. When the mountain Indians left their territory during the winter to go to their desert homes, the cattlemen claimed the "abandoned" areas as their own. The Indians believed that no man owned land, "...but the white man and Spanish thought differently. Well, you can't go up against gun powder with bow and arrow." Prior to 1846, Spanish and Mexican land grants took Indian lands.

Tom's father, Adolf Lugo, was trying to organize the Indians so that they might have recourse against the local cattlemen. With rumors of a threat against his life, he was forced to leave his wife and son and return to his former home in Cahuilla territory (Adolf Lugo was a *Kwaaymii* but was orphaned very young. He was raised by distant Cahuilla relatives).

Life was not easy for the Indians during these times. On one hand missionaries were condemning them for their beliefs. On the other, the ranchers were taking over their homelands.

During the next few years, the *Kwaaymii* found they could no longer support themselves as they had been accustomed to doing in the past. Eventually a few found jobs working at the missions and for individual families. Tom's great uncle, Istaako (brother of SuSaan), worked on the Butterfield Stage Road, where he earned tools for pay. With those tools he built the cabin that would be Tom's birthplace nearly fifty years later. Pedro Kwamaay, Tom's maternal grandfather, worked at the San Diego Mission tending the olive trees and gardens and also learning the gold and silversmith trade.

The land grabbing continued. The Indians still went to their winter homes in the desert but a few always stayed behind to protect their mountain territory. It was a useless battle for them. The cattlemen put the congressmen in office and the congressmen voted to allot more lands to the cattlemen. "You know, the big land grabbers and all of that time didn't want

Tom's father, Adolf Lugo, holding his granddaughter, Jackie, 1933.

the Indians educated. They say if you educate the Indians, that's a mighty weapon in their hands. And these land grabbers, they don't want to be exposed. They were doing a lot of crooked work. They kept grabbing up as much land as they could of the Indians and they had their congressmen working for them too. They tried everything to retard the Indians' growth."

In 1891, the Mission Indian Commission, composed of C. C. Painter, A. K. Smiley and Joseph B. Moore, was to investigate the landless condition and to determine the numbers and areas of the Indians so that lands could be allotted to them. But it seems the cattlemen had their way again, because there were many people and villages that were not reported. The ranchers got more land. The Indian was forced to conform to the white man's way of life, but had no rights whatsoever. Once the reservation lands had been determined, the Indians were expected to stay on them.

The right section of Maria's house was the first segment built by Tom's great uncle, Istaako about 1850. The new addition at left was built about 1875.

The newer addition at right. Tom is standing in the doorway of the section in which he was born. Standing outside are his grandmother, SuSaan, and his mother, Maria. c. 1913.

Tom holds the log splitter that his great uncle used to build the cabin in which Tom was born.

Section of old Butterfield Stage Road in Box Canyon. Tom's great uncle, Istaako, worked on this road.

Tom stands in the ruins of the old cabin where he was born.

It would seem that the plight of the California Indian was a fateful one. After hundreds of years of relatively uneventful change, they were plummeted into the hectic onslaught of "modern civilization." Unfortunately, the knowledge and talents of the Native American were pushed aside by the intruders, and every stand the Indians took was considered an act of aggression against the whites. Defending the encroachment the only way they knew brought on them the label of "savage." Having no recourse through government channels only forced them into their own kind of retaliation.

The cry of "gold" in 1848 brought hoards of settlers into California. Little by little, as more gold was discovered, the arm of the new American frontier extended further into aboriginal settlements, usurping valuable plots which had been previously inhabited. After two years of the continuing invasion, it looked like there was finally some relief in sight for the Indians. President Millard Fillmore appointed three Commissioners in 1850 for the purpose of making treaties with the California tribes. The Commissioners were conscientious enough in their efforts to relocate the Indians on to

127

suitable lands—areas in which they could continue to pursue their cultural life styles. They agreed to eighteen treaties which the Commissioners then submitted to the U.S. Senate for approval. But California settlers were concerned about the Indians getting reservations in rich mining areas, and the Senators, voting with their constituents in mind, rejected all eighteen treaties. The valuable mining lands were wide open to the settlers' claims and the Indians were back in square one.

Times were very tough for the native Californian for many years. They survived as best they could under the circumstances. Fortunately, during the following years, there were a number of individuals—some very influential ones—who befriended them and were willing to extend a helping hand to the floundering Indian communities. After a long, hard struggle, the Indians finally won their citizenship rights—in 1924.

Chapter IX

MISCELLANEOUS

Medicine

ANYONE COULD PREPARE and use the plants listed here without the aid of a shaman.

Bayberry and eucalyptus—The leaves are used to make a tea for the treatment of cough or congestion. In another use, the leaves were put in a pot of hot water and the sick person would sit over the pot completely covered with a blanket which served as a tent to contain the vapors that he inhaled. Of course, the eucalyptus leaves were not used until modern times, when the railroad companies planted large groves in Southern California.

Creosote bush—A tea was made from the leaves of this bush. It is very bitter tasting but works well to relieve symptoms of influenza. Mr. Lucas says it was widely used among the Indians in the 1918 influenza epidemic. "You live a thousand deaths just drinking that stuff...but it sure works."

Chokecherry—They dried this fruit, which could be stored indefinitely. When boiled it made a sour tasting drink about the color of coffee. It was used to settle an upset stomach and to purify the blood.

Jimson weed—A poultice made with the leaves of this plant mixed with goose fat was used to put on cuts or bad scrapes. For more on the uses of this plant for religious purposes, see section on Puberty Rites.

Color Symbolism

"Red is always symbolic of life and energy and blood. Blue is a quite sacred color because it tells of the kingdom of *Amaayahaa* [the Great Spirit], the heavens above and the ruler of all the earth. It's very hard to get a true color like that. That's why the Indians went for any stones that color, like the turquoise. We never had turquoise out here except by trading. Yellow is always cheerful and sunny, bright. Black represents morbid despair. That's why, in the early days, when people lose their relatives and are mourning, crying, reminiscing over things, they usually paint in streaks on their faces the black graphite. If they don't have the black rock, they use ashes mixed with tallow. Any stranger coming along realizes right away their state, and sympathizes with them instead of just talking, passing the time of day. White represents clearness of thought, mentally and spiritually. Brown doesn't have a particular meaning. It's referred to as *amat kwakwas* [the brown earth]. Green is symbolic of any growth, anything that's coming up—young, tender, new life, new leaves. Along the rivers you find the watercress, the mustard greens and especially wild clover greens. That was very much thought of."

Fumigation

When the *Kwaaymii* returned to the mountains in the spring, they fumigated their houses. They built a small fire inside the house and put sage, wild cantaloupe or bay leaves on the fire. The smoke and fumes drove out spiders, insects or just about anything that had moved into the dwelling during the winter. They also fumigated a house whenever anyone had been sick for a long time. The plant that was preferred was the wild cantaloupe, which was not always available. Sage was the second choice.

Soap

The *Kwaaymii* used the root of the Spanish dagger plant (a species of yucca) to make soap for washing hair. They took a small piece of the root and boiled it in water. When it had cooled, they strained it into a small olla and it could be stored for two to three weeks before it would spoil. As Mr. Lucas puts it, "I'll tell you, your hair whistles it's so clean." In the old days they used ashes, which was very rough on the hair because of the lye content.

Brooms

These were generally made from the cambium of cedar bark. The fiber was very fine, but stiff, and was dried out on a platform then tied in a bundle with a handle attached. A few brooms were made with tufts of pine needles but they didn't last too long because the needles broke easily when they dried out. A type of whiskbroom of pine needles was used to brush ground seeds from mortars.

Manners

Greediness at meals or helping oneself first was considered bad manners. Whatever was picked up first was always offered to someone else. People always took food with them when visiting. No one was supposed to just "drop in" at mealtime. Consideration of others was important to the *Kwaaymii*.

Shaving

They used two pieces of bone like tweezers to pull the hair out. *Kwaaymii* men had little hair on their faces and bodies.

APPENDICES

Word Pronunciation Key

a	*ahaa*	as in alone, sofa
aa	*Enyaa*	as in father
ch	*nyanyawich*	as in church
e	*atiiyech*	as in pet
h	*parhaw*	as in house
i	*ishpaa*	as in pin, stick
ii	*pariiwii*	as in meet, see
k	*akwak*	as in kick
l	*sonaal*	as in lieu
m	*nesom*	as in mother
n	*sinyaw*	as in no
nn	*wamunn*	as in win
o	*sopit*	as in for
p	*sarap*	as in flip
r	*aakwer*	as in bear
rr	*aakuurr*	as in Sp. rio, very slight trill (rare)
s	*lemis*	as in soap, miss
t	*otup*	as in Tom, pelt
tl	*Kwatatl*	as in kettle
u	*winuk*	as in foot, put, look
uu	*waauuut*	as in boot, food
w	*porwer*	as in water
y	*yeryer*	as in yes
´	*nyam´aay*	catch or hesitation between syllables
aw	*parhaw*	as in how
ay	*amayhwann*	as in say (rare)
aay	*Kwaaymii*	as in aisle, eye
iw	*chapsiw*	as in few (rare)
oy	*waahoyp*	as in boy (rare)

Pental-Decimal Counting System

The *Kwaaymii*, as well as many other aboriginal groups, had no reason to develop an elaborate counting system. For instance, they had no concept of the number of miles it was between one place or another. They simply figured how many days it took them to walk to where they wanted to go. It was not 100 miles to them, but a four or five day journey; not 365 days in a year, but twelve or thirteen moons; not several hundred people living in a village, but a large village with a major chief and full council; not 85 years old, but born many, many summers ago. As a result, they did not need the larger numbers which we need today.

Tom Lucas recalls the Indian words for numbers up to sixty. Based on the structure of 10, with the substructure of 5, one could extrapolate this counting system to 99. The *Kwaaymii* had no word for 100.

1	*asin*
2	*hawak*
3	*hamak*
4	*chapap*
5	*sarap*
6	*sarap amaayk asin* (5 plus 1)
7	*sarap amaayk hawak*
8	*sarap amaayk hamak*
9	*sarap amaayk chapap*
10	*shahok*
11	*shahok amaayk asin* (10 plus 1)
12	*shahok amaayk hawak*
13	*shahok amaayk hamak*
14	*shahok amaayk chapap*
15	*shahok amaayk sa rap*
16	*shahok sarap amaayk asin* (10-5 plus 1)
17	*shahok sarap amaayk hawak*
18	*shahok sarap amaayk hamak*
19	*shahok sa rap amaayk chapap*
20	*mii hawak*
21	*mii hawak amaayk asin* (20 plus 1)

22 *mii hawak amaayk hawak*
23 *mii hawak amaayk hamak*
24 *mii hawak amaayk chapap*
25 *mii hawak amaayk sarap*
26 *mii hawak sarap amaayk asin* (20-5 plus 1)
27 *mii hawak sa rap amaayk hawak*
28 *mii hawak sa rap amaayk hamak*
29 *mii hawak sa rap amaayk chapap*
30 *mii hamak*
31 *mii hamak amaayk asin*
32 *mii hamak amaayk hawak*
33 *mii hamak amaayk hamak*
34 *mii hamak amaayk chapap*
35 *mii hamak amaayk sarap*
36 *mii hamak sa rap amaayk asin*
37 *mii hamak sarap amaayk hawak*
38 *mii hamak sarap amaayk hamak*
39 *mii hamak sa rap amaayk chapap*
40 *mii chapap*
41 *mii chapap amaayk asin*
42 *mii chapap amaayk hawak*
43 *mii chapap amaayk hamak*
44 *mii chapap amaayk chapap*
45 *mii chapap amaayk sarap*
46 *mii chapap sa rap amaayk asin*
47 *mii chapap sarap amaayk hawak*
48 *mii chapap sarap amaayk hamak*
49 *mii chapap sarap amaayk chapap*
50 *mii sa rap*
51 *mii sa rap amaayk asin*
52 *mii sarap amaayk hawak*
53 *mii sa rap amaayk hamak*
54 *mii sarap amaayk chapap*
55 *mii sarap amaayk sarap*
56 *mii sarap sarap amaayk asin*
57 *mii sarap sarap amaayk hawak*
58 *mii sarap sa rap amaayk hamak*
59 *mii sarap sarap amaayk chapap*
60 *mii sarap amaayk shahok* (50 plus 10)

70	*mii sarap amaayk mii hawak* (50 + 20 extrapolated)
80	*mii sa rap amaayk mii hamak* (50 + 30 extrapolated)
90	*mii sarap amaayk mii chapap* (50 + 40 extrapolated)

Flora

Arrowweed	*Pluchea sericea*
Bamboo, mountain	unidentified
Barrel cactus	*Ferocactus cylindraceus*
Bayberry	*Umbellularia califomica*
Beavertail cactus	*Opuntia basilaris*
Castor bean	*Ricinus communis*
Cat-tail	*Typha latifolia*
Cedar	*Calocedrus decurrens*
Celery, wild	unidentified
Century plant	*Agave deserti*
Chamise	*Adenostoma fasciculatum*
Chia	*Salvia columbariae*
Chokecherry	*Prunus virginiana*
Clover	*Trifolium* sp.
Creosote bush	*Larrea tridentate*
Cypress	*Cupressus stephensonii*
Deergrass	*Muhlenbergia rigens*
Elderberry	*Sambucus Mexicana*
Eucalyptus	*Eucalyptus* sp.
Gourd	*Cucurbita foetidissima*
Honeysuckle	*Lonicera subspicata*
Huckleberry	*Vaccinium ovatum*
Ironwood	*Olneya tesota*
Jimson weed	*Datura meteloides*
Juniper	*Juniperus califomica*
Lilac	*Ceanothus* sp.
Mesquite	*Prosopis glandulosa*
Milkweed	*Asclepias* sp.
Mint	unidentified
Mustard	*Brassica* sp.
Oak, black	*Quercus kelloggii*
Oak, live	*Quercus agrifolia*

Pine, pinyon	*Pinus monophylla*
Pine, ponderosa	*Pinus jeffreyi,* and *Pinus ponderosa*
Pumpkin	*Cucurbita pepo*
Reed	*Phragmites australis*
Sage, white	*Salvia apiana*
Sagebrush	*Artemisia tridentata*
Spanish dagger or bayonet	*Yucca schidigera*
Tobacco, coyote	*Nicotiana attenuata*
Tule	*Juncus textilis*
Watercress	*Rorippa nasturtium-aquaticum*
Willow	*Salix* sp.
Witch hazel	*Rhus trilobata*
Yerba santa	*Eriodictyon trichocalyx*
Yucca	*Yucca schidigera*

Calendar

Moon Phases

First quarter – *hillyaa top uk,* also *puywach*

Full moon – *hillyaa taamur*

Third quarter – *hillya waam*

New moon – *hillyaa nyahuun,* also *hillyaa mutl'aay* (dead moon)

Eclipse

Lunar eclipse – *hillyaay wisaw,* means moon being eaten. During an eclipse, medicine men from all surrounding tribes gathered for meditation from which they brought prophecies to their people.

Solar eclipse – *enyaa karuk,* means a spiritual disappearance of the sun. There is no literal translation for a solar eclipse.

Months

The *Kwaaymii* acknowledged four divisions of the year.

January, February – *saa'ii* (buzzard) or *hiichur* (cold)

March, April, May – *chiipam* (getting out, warmer)

June, July, August – *iipall* (hot)

September, October, November, December – *kapaw* (work time—everybody and everything)

Petroglyphs

When asked about petroglyphs, Tom offered the drawings and explanations given below.

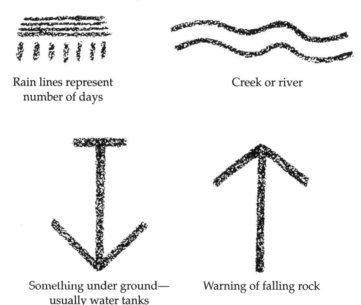

Rain lines represent
number of days

Creek or river

Something under ground—
usually water tanks

Warning of falling rock

Day and night

BIBLIOGRAPHY

Anderson, George E., W. H. Ellison and Robert F. Heizer

1978   *Treaty Making and Treaty Rejection by the Federal Government in California, 1850-1852*. Ballena Press, Socorro, New Mexico.

Beatty, Donald R.

1957   *History of the Legal Status of the American Indian with Particular Reference to California*. A thesis, University of Southern California, R&E Research Associates.

Davis, James

1961   *Trade Routes and Economic Exchange Among the Indians of California*. University of California Archaeological Survey, Report No. 54, Berkeley. Gifford, E. W.

1918   *Clans and Moieties in Southern California*. University of California Publications in American Archaeology and Ethnology, Vol. 14.

1931   *The Kamia of Imperial Valley*. Smithsonian Institution, Bureau of American Ethnology, Bulletin 97, Washington, D.C.

Hedges, Ken

1975   *Notes on the Kumeyaay: A Problem of Identification*. The Journal of California Anthropology, Summer 1975, Vol. 2, No. 1.

Heizer, Robert F.

1978   *California, Vol. 8 in Handbook of the North American Indians*. Smithsonian Institution, Washington, D.C.

Johnson, Mary Elizabeth

1914   *Indian Legends of the Cuyamaca Mountains*. M. E. Johnson.

Kroeber, A. L.

1925   *Handbook of the Indians of California.* Dover
        Publications, Inc., New York.

1974   *Selected Writings of Kroeber on Land Use and
        Political Organization of California Indians.*
        American Indian Ethnohistory, California
        Indians IV, Garland Publishing, Inc., New York.

Lounsbury, Ralph G.

1974   *Records of Mexican Land Claims in California.*
        American Indian Ethnohistory, California
        Indians IV, Garland Publishing, Inc., New York.

Moriarty, James R.

1968   *The Environmental Variations of the Yuman Culture
        Area in Southern California.* Quarterly Bulletin of
        the Anthropological Association of Canada,
        Part I, Vol. 6, No. 2; Part II, Vol. 6, No. 3.

Munz, Philip A.

1974   *A Flora of Southern California.* University of
        California Press, Berkeley.

Pourade, Richard F.

1961   *Time of the Bells—The History of San Diego.* The
        Union Tribune Publishing Company, San Diego,
        California.

Reed, Lester

1967   *Old Timers of Southeastern California.* Lester Reed,
        California.

Rogers, Malcolm J.

1936   *Yuman Pottery Making.* San Diego Museum
        Papers 2, Ballena Press, Ramona, California.

1945   *An Outline of Yuman Prehistory.* Southwestern
        Journal of Anthropology, Vol. 1, No. 2.

1966   *Ancient Hunters of the Far West.* The Union
        Tribune Publishing Company, San Diego,
        California.

Spencer, R. F. and J. D. Jennings, et al.

    1965   *The Native Americans.* Harper and Row, New
              York.

Strong, William Duncan

    1929   *Aboriginal Society in Southern California.*
              University of California Publication in American
              Archaeology and Ethnology, Vol. 26, Berkeley.

Young, James R.

    n.d.   *The Creation and Administrative History of the Pala*
              Indian Reservation from 1865 to the Present.